The Lampstand Prison Ministry: Constructed On Catholic Social Teaching & the History of the Catholic Church

By David H. Lukenbill

2

The Lampstand Prison
Ministry: Constructed On
Catholic Social Teaching
& the History of the
Catholic Church

By

David H. Lukenbill

A Chulu Press Book

First Chulu Press Edition published

December 2011

ISBN-10: 0-9791670-8-6
ISBN-13: 978-0-9791670-8-9

Published by The Lampstand Foundation

www.lampstandfoundation.org

To Marlene and Erika, who always understood, and to Joe and Kathleen, who were always there.

Contents

Preface

The foundational ideas animating the Lampstand prison ministry—that it takes a reformed criminal to reform criminals and that the conversion approach must be intellectual—are ideas I have been working with since the beginning of my reformation from criminality at age thirty five, as I began seeing the world from the perspective of a college education (leading to a successful criminal rehabilitative college-based educational program I developed and managed) and continuing to the final washing from my spirit the last remnants of a lifetime of criminal thinking twenty years later, in the waters of baptism.

The peer relationship is where the impact this apostolate may have on future criminal activity lies, and it will be seen most dramatically within the Lampstand prison ministry where the apostolate work will *only* be optimized by conversions of the criminal/carceral elite—the professional criminal—whose history within rehabilitative work is virtually nil, because for him, the rewards of deep immersion within the criminal/carceral culture are too great, and other than as a ruse, rehabilitation is considered a tragic fool's errand.

Prison ministry has traditionally been done as a corporal work of mercy, a Catholic

Worker no-means-test approach, and the results—considering the recidivism rate of about 70% nationally—has not been very good.

The Lampstand prison ministry views prison ministry as a spiritual work of mercy using a means-tested approach.

Benestad (2011) comments on the three spiritual works of mercy most congruent with the Lampstand prison ministry, in relation to being a Good Samaritan.

> It is noteworthy that three of the spiritual works of mercy (Counsel the doubtful, Instruct the ignorant, and Admonish sinners) pertain to the communication of truth, thereby implying that being in error is a form of suffering. So, leading people to the truth by way of evangelization, for example, is a work of the Good Samaritan. (p. 54)

To the professional criminal "being in error" is most certainly a form of suffering, for the worldview underlying his criminality is built on "knowing".

The corporal works of mercy with prisoners has individual application with little optimizational benefit, while the spiritual works of mercy—though also of individual application—have great benefit.

The difference is in who is ministered to. The traditional prison ministry works with any and all prisoners, while the Lampstand ministry, wanting to amplify its work, focuses exclusively on professional criminals—those who commit crimes for money, and who are not informants, pedophiles, or rapists—as the professional criminals are those most apt to have success evangelizing other prisoners due to their criminal/carceral credibility.

Regarding informants, it is important to remember that when a criminal truly has an internal transformation and converts to religious belief where justice becomes a singular personal aspect of his spirituality; if at that point he reveals to authorities the nature and involvement of himself and others in crimes crying out for justice—rather than for a personal reward in reduced sanctions for criminal acts—he would be acting in good faith and criminals would not necessarily condemn him, but the informant who only acts for reward, criminals will always condemn.

The criminal/carceral world is a tightly closed culture in which personal character and reputation are known nationwide due to the prison cultural grapevine's effectiveness, and the ability of professional criminals who have been converted, to convert other criminals is amplified, due to their high status and reputation for constancy, which does not apply to informants, pedophiles, or rapists.

In liberal Catholic narratives, the way of evil in the world is largely ignored, as if it did not exist. Liberal Catholics believe they can practice pacifism in the face of war and pacifism's criminal justice cousin, restorative justice, in the face of criminal evil. They believe they can abolish capital punishment and use psychotherapy to counsel rapists and pedophiles. They act as if love conquers all—the great misreading of Catholic tradition and scripture. The only love that does conquer all, is God's love for us and within the fire of that love resides the tempered steel of the sword of justice, the sword St. Michael the Archangel has wielded since time immemorial, driving Satan from Heaven and protecting the Church; reminding us of its efficacy in the hands of the Catholic Crusaders, the warrior monks who protected Christendom for centuries and whose need is ever more acute today; if not with steel swords—though those wielded by saints and angels should never be beaten into plowshares lest the innocent be plowed into dirt by evil men—with the fire tempered *Word*.

Principles of traditional martial Catholic thinking on criminal justice issues have rarely seen wide discussion throughout the Church and have largely lain fallow for some time, at least since the papacy of Pius XII.

Since then there has been little thinking around criminal justice.

Many Catholic thinkers reflecting on criminals begin with the assumption—wonderfully well-intentioned but woefully naïve to the way of evil in the world and how deeply evil has captured many human souls—that the criminal is Christ.

In the words and actions of Christ, this idea finds spare root, for what did he say about Judas, that "it would have been better for that man if he had not been born" (Matthew 26:24).

And what did he say about those who harm children. "...but whoever causes one of these little ones who believe in me to sin, it would be better for him to have a great millstone fastened round his neck and to be drowned in the depth of the sea." (Matthew-18:6)

This tradition of seeing Christ in criminals by many Catholics working in prison ministry can be troublesome, as the reality is more complex, as Maritain (1968) wrote:

> To see Jesus in our brothers is an abridged formula, and one which could be misunderstood. Did not, however, Jesus make himself one with them, did he not make all their sorrows his own? "I was hungry and you gave me food, I was thirsty and you gave me to drink, I was a stranger, and you welcomed me, I was naked and you clothed me, I was sick and you visited me; I was in prison and you came to me" (*Matthew* 25:35). That is true, but the fact remains that our brothers are mere creatures, confronting our eyes, and not (to us who have not had the chance to see Him with our eyes) God before the gaze of our soul, as is Jesus when we contemplate him in his very humanity.

It is not exactly *in them*, it is rather through them and *behind them* that we see Jesus and his love for them. And by the same token, it is *in arrear* of our attention to others, and of our exchanges with them, in arrear of the noise they make and we make, it is an inner silence in which the spiritual preconscious much more than the conscious is absorbed, that our soul is attracted to Jesus who is there, and to his love for our brothers, who are his brothers. And this inner silence in us— which the man who speaks to us perceives also in a manner much more unconscious that conscious—is no doubt the best part of what he receives from our so much disarmed fraternal charity.

To contemplate, alone with Him alone, God in the humanity of Jesus; and to contemplate Jesus through our neighbor, whom he loves and whom we love—these are the two most highly desirable paths of contemplation for a man engaged in the labors of the world. But neither is easy for him. (p. 237)

The Church teaches us that we *are capable of entering into communion* with our neighbor and we *are called by grace* to a covenant with God, but Satan has a *certain dominion over us and our nature is wounded and inclined to evil.*

As a consequence, for the penitential criminal, our entire life will be on the battlefield and many will fall. To persevere and win the eternal, we must be armored of God and we must *struggle to do what is right.*

357 Being in the image of God the human individual possesses the dignity of a person, who is not just something, but someone. **He is capable** of self-knowledge, of self-possession and of freely giving himself and entering into communion with other persons. And he is **called by grace** to a covenant with his Creator, to offer him a response of faith and love that no other creature can give in his stead.

407 The doctrine of original sin, closely connected with that of redemption by Christ, provides lucid discernment of man's situation and activity in the world. By our first parents' sin, the devil has acquired **a certain domination over man**, even though man remains free. Original sin entails "captivity under the power of him who thenceforth had the power of death, that is, the devil". Ignorance of the fact that **man has a wounded nature inclined to evil** gives rise to serious errors in the areas of education, politics, social action and morals.

408 The consequences of original sin and of all men's personal sins put the world as a whole in the sinful condition aptly described in St. John's expression, "the sin of the world". This expression can also refer to the negative influence exerted on people by communal situations and social structures that are the fruit of men's sins.

409 This dramatic situation of "the whole world [which] is in the power of the evil one" makes man's life a battle:

> The whole of man's history has been the story of dour combat with the powers of evil, stretching, so our Lord tells us, from the very dawn of history until the last day. Finding himself in the midst of the battlefield man has to struggle to do what is right, and it is at great cost to himself, and aided by God's grace, that he succeeds in achieving his own inner integrity. (*Catechism of the Catholic Church* #357 & #407-409) (Highlighting added)

For the criminal, the beginning of that long and arduous battle is true penance and a transformation that will be remarked on by others, even the guards in his prison, and this penance will be carried in a struggling grasp for the rest of our lives.

Though we have received the forgiveness of baptism and our past has been cleansed, it will sometimes haunt us when the evil we have done surges up in our memory, drawn by a remembrance of the past triggered by an event in the present and this is how it should be, for the wages of our evil done, though cleansed, has marked our soul, and we can best continue to salve those scars through our apostolate helping evangelize other criminals.

Evil exists and it exists most potently within prisons, and that is an arena of the most dangerous apostolate work, which only the Catholic Church can effectively carry out, by virtue of her ancient truth and the promise embedded in her founding words: "And I say to thee: That thou art Peter; and upon this rock I will build my church, and the gates of hell shall not prevail against it." (Matthew 16:18)

Each human being, including criminals, has within him an instinctual reaching for the supernatural—a divine invitation—but for those who do not encounter the truth of the Catholic Church in a form full enough and orthodox enough to call forth their response, there are an endless array of worldly lures promising a false supernatural aspect, and within the criminal world these lures are dark, deep, and powerfully alluring; reaching back into ancient pagan history and cult to call the criminal to the endless feast of power, money, intoxication, and sensuality.

Aquinas teaches us about the divine invitation from the perspective of the believer:

> The believer has sufficient motive for believing, for he is moved by the authority of Divine teaching confirmed by miracles, and, what is more, by the inward instinct of the Divine invitation... (*Summa Theologica,* Pt. II-II, Q. 2 Art. 9)

But for the unbeliever, it is crucial that Catholic truth be revealed in a way and from a source from which he can open himself to the Divine invitation.

It is hoped that this work and all of the work of the Lampstand Foundation, will, along with the works of the other—though far too few—Catholics working in this field, add to a renewal of prison apostolate work, this vital ministry, for in the call from Christ to visit him in prison, it was also an individual call from the Cross, to help the Good Thief, for Christ extends to each of us the Divine Invitation, *Follow Me.*

Introduction

Professional criminals want, most of all, to not be taken as they take others, to not be robbed, thieved, burgled, conned or otherwise snookered about the truths of life, about which they are certain, in their choice of criminality, that they have mastered, along with its obviously congruent carceral world; and if they discover that there is another hidden world—for the truths of the criminal/carceral world are also deeply hidden—where a truth trumps his, as Christ's truth trumped Dismas' on Golgotha, he will grasp hold of it as surely as cash available to his quick hands.

The prison ministry in this book is designed for an individual Catholic parish working with a maximum security prison, through a ministry community of at least four parishioners, in conjunction with the prison's Catholic priest, and supported by prison officials.

In order for a Catholic parish to effectively provide a prison ministry that can lead to conversion, a new paradigm in thinking about the criminal world is required rather than the Hollywood dramas or Marxist fantasies too often animating many undertaking this most valuable of ministries called for by Christ in his final teaching to the apostles.

31 "When the Son of Man comes in his glory, and all the angels with him, he will sit upon his glorious throne, **32** and all the nations will be assembled before him. And he will separate them one from another, as a shepherd separates the sheep from the goats. **33** He will place the sheep on his right and the goats on his left. **34** Then the king will say to those on his right, 'Come, you who are blessed by my Father. Inherit the kingdom prepared for you from the foundation of the world. **35** For I was hungry and you gave me food, I was thirsty and you gave me drink, a stranger and you welcomed me, **36** naked and you clothed me, ill and you cared for me, in prison and you visited me.' **37** Then the righteous will answer him and say, 'Lord, when did we see you hungry and feed you, or thirsty and give you drink? **38** When did we see you a stranger and welcome you, or naked and clothe you? **39** When did we see you ill or in prison, and visit you?' **40** And the king will say to them in reply, 'Amen, I say to you, whatever you did for one of these least brothers of mine, you did for me.' **41** Then he will say to those on his left, 'Depart from me, you accursed, into the eternal fire prepared for the devil and his angels. **42** For I was hungry and you gave me no food, I was thirsty and you gave me

no drink, **43** a stranger and you gave
me no welcome, naked and you gave me
no clothing, ill and in prison, and you
did not care for me.' **44** Then they will
answer and say, 'Lord, when did we see
you hungry or thirsty or a stranger or
naked or ill or in prison, and not
minister to your needs?' **45** He will
answer them, 'Amen, I say to you, what
you did not do for one of these least
ones, you did not do for me.' **46** And
these will go off to eternal punishment,
but the righteous to eternal life."
(Matthew 25: 31-46)

The greatest of these needs is the
spiritual, for the prisoner, having willingly
entered Satan's snare anticipating worldly
rewards, has been captured by the prince of
this world, and it is only through the weapons
of spiritual warfare—learned from the social
teaching of the Church—that he can free
himself, weapons which the Catholic prison
minister can help bring to him.

Pope John Paul II (1991) writes of the
power of the social teaching.

The Encyclical *Rerum novarum* can be
read as a valid contribution to socio-
economic analysis at the end of the
nineteenth century, but its specific
value derives from the fact that it is a
document of the Magisterium and is
fully a part of the Church's evangelizing

mission, together with many other documents of this nature. Thus the Church's *social teaching* is itself a valid *instrument of evangelization*. As such, it proclaims God and his mystery of salvation in Christ to every human being, and for that very reason reveals man to himself. In this light, and only in this light, does it concern itself with everything else: the human rights of the individual, and in particular of the "working class", the family and education, the duties of the State, the ordering of national and international society, economic life, culture, war and peace, and respect for life from the moment of conception until death. (#54)

Maritain, R. (1936) writes about the prince of this world and the power of Our Lord that can "destroy his principality."

A star that shone but an instant in the firmament of grace, falling, he became darkness and "ruler of the darkness of this world." ...

It becomes him, also, to haunt this world: God allows it him, because it is good that every spirit should be tried...

The treacherous angel recovers in part, through the sin of Adam, what he lost by his own sin. He reconquers by a new title his dominion not indeed over the whole order of nature, but over sinful man and over material creation in so far as it is man's domain and may serve sin. He infests innocent fountains, hills, woods; he hides himself in the storm. He holds sway over people and their civilization; sacrifices are offered to him; for him men commit their children to the flames. (pp. 3-5)

The pierced hands of the Son are needed to loose the merciful hands of the Father, held captive by our sins, to put in bonds the Prince of this world and destroy his principality. (*Ibid.* pp. 12-13)

Though the prince of this world is powerful and, in many cases can draw men into sin, he is not the cause of every sin, as Aquinas (1948) teaches.

But a thing is said to be the direct cause of something, when its action tends directly thereunto. And in this way the devil is not the cause of every sin: for all sins are not committed at the devil's instigation, but some are due to the free-will and the corruption of the flesh. For, as Origen says...even if there were no devil, men would have the desire for food and love and such like pleasures;

25

with regard to which many disorders may arise unless those desires be curbed by reason, especially if we presuppose the corruption of our natures. Now it is in the power of the free-will to curb this appetite and keep it in order. Consequently there is no need for all sins to be due to the instigation of the devil. But those sins which are due thereto man perpetuates *"through being deceived by the same blandishments as were our first parents"* (Pt. 1, Q. 114, Art. 3, Answer.)

The criminal world is a vast and ancient cultural entity—stretching back to the reign of the first criminal, Cain, and his building of the city of man wherein criminality rules—that traditionally was largely isolated within local or national boundaries, but which over the past several decades has become global, noted by Sterling (1994):

> International organized crime, an imaginary menace for many in 1990, was a worldwide emergency by 1993. The big syndicates of East and West were pooling services and personnel, rapidly colonizing Western Europe and the United States, running the drug traffic up to half a trillion dollars a year, laundering and reinvesting an estimated quarter of a trillion dollars a year in legitimate enterprise. Much of

their phenomenal growth derived from the fact that they had the free run of a territory covering half the continent of Europe and a good part of Asia—a sixth of the earth's land mass, essentially ungoverned and unpoliced.

The whole international underworld had moved in on post-communist Russia and the rest of the ex-Soviet bloc: raced in from the day the Berlin Wall fell. Where Western governments tended to see Russia as a basket case, the big syndicates saw it as a privileged sanctuary and bottomless source of instant wealth. (p. 14)

Within this paradigm of a global criminal world connected through opportune action, prisons play a crucial role—especially in the United States—for it is in prison that the forging of criminal leadership is most dramatically developed, tested, and refined, and it is there that the greatest need for the work of the Church to minister to criminals enmeshed by the deepest evil, exists.

The same forces driving the paradigmatic clash of civilizations are driving criminal world cultural development, where internal ideology is the governor, and power and control of turf is the result and only the power of the social teaching of the Church can thwart it.

What is missing from the works on prison ministry I've studied is an understanding of the underlying criminal/carceral world narrative which animates professional criminality. Without addressing this and without daily sacramental practice—putting on the armor of God—by the prison minister, most professed prison conversions are as shallow as rain on the window pane.

The eternal reason criminals are criminals is because they are distant from God, and that is a result—as it is for all of us—of their individual choice, and crime as choice is the sociological province of criminal justice/public policy expert, James Q. Wilson.

Part of the reason that he is described by Jenkins (2011) as "America's greatest thinker on crime, punishment and social order" is *because* of the crime as choice theory described in Wilson's (1985) magisterial work with Richard J. Herrnstein, *Crime & Human Nature.*

> Our theory rests on the assumption that people, when faced with a choice, choose the preferred course of action. This assumption is quite weak; it says nothing more than that whatever people choose to do, they choose it because they prefer it. In fact, it is more than weak; without further clarification, it is a tautology. When we say people "choose," we do not necessarily mean

that they consciously deliberate about what to do. All we mean is that their behavior is determined by its consequences. A person will do that thing the consequences of which are perceived by him or her to be preferable to the consequences of doing something else. What can save such a statement from being a tautology is how plausibly we describe the gains and losses associated with alternative courses of action and the standards by which a person evaluates those gains and losses.

These assumptions are commonplace in philosophy and social science. Philosophers speak of hedonism or utilitarianism, economists of value or utility, and psychologists of reinforcement or reward. We will use the language of psychology, but it should not be hard to translate our terminology into that of other disciplines. Though social scientists differ as to how much behavior can reasonably be described as the result of a choice, all agree that at least some behavior is guided, or even precisely controlled, by things variously termed pleasure, pain, happiness, sorrow, desirability, or the like. Our object is to show how this simple and widely used idea can be used to explain behavior.

At any given moment, a person can choose between committing a crime and not committing it (all these alternatives to crime we lump together as "noncrime"). The consequences of committing the crime consists of rewards (what psychologists call "reinforcers") and punishments; the consequences of not committing the crime (i.e., engaging in noncrime) also entail gains and losses. The larger the ratio of the net rewards of crime to the net rewards of noncrime, the greater the tendency to commit the crime. The net rewards of crime include, obviously, the likely material gains from the crime, but they also include intangible benefits, such as obtaining emotional or sexual gratification, receiving the approval of peers, satisfying an old score against an enemy, or enhancing one's sense of justice. One must deduct from these rewards of crime any losses that accrue immediately—that are, so to speak, contemporaneous with the crime. They include the pangs of conscience, the disapproval of onlookers, and the retaliation of the victim. (pp. 43-44)

Maritain (1996) comments on the freedom of the person in relation to God:

A person is a universe of spiritual nature endowed with freedom of choice and constituting to this extent a whole which is independent in face of the world—neither nature nor the State can lay hold of the universe without its permission. And God himself, who is and acts within, acts there in a particular manner and with a particularly exquisite delicacy, which shows the value He sets on it: He respects its freedom, at the heart of which He nevertheless lives; He solicits it, He never forces it. (p. 158)

The Lampstand prison ministry is partially animated by the axiomatic criminal and carceral world principle of *walking the talk*—so clearly tied to accepting individual responsibility for individual choices—by studying who the Church *says* she is through her social teaching, in relation to *who* she was throughout her history.

The ministry is also built upon the foundation of family that characterized our Lord's mission on earth—where his cousin John the Baptist and his good friend Lazarus, and Lazarus's sister Mary Magdalene, played such an important role—the family that presents the ministry is the parish and from the parish family will come the strength and love that will carry this ministry through the dark and dangerous days ahead to the great light upon Catholic truth it will shine.

Construction

With Peter, to Christ, through Mary, shows us the path.

Peter stumbled (and as the prototype of all popes throughout history, stumbles still) denying Christ thrice and like the other apostles, save John, and Mary Magdalene—who tradition calls "Apostle to the Apostles" for her delivering the message of Christ's Resurrection to the other Apostles—ran away during the central event of the God-Man's ministry, the crucifixion, leaving only John and Magdalene with the Virgin Mother and the other Mary at the foot of the cross.

The ministry lesson here is not to base our faith on individuals whether laity, priests or popes, but on the sacred doctrine of the Church and the Church Triumphant which grows in eternity, and by using her social teaching which began in the beginning with Genesis, hand in hand with her history.

John was the most powerfully spiritual and intellectual of the apostles and Magdalene was a penitential and transformed criminal, while the other apostles and disciples were more representative of the people; fishermen, tax collector, doctor.

There were then two criminals, Dismas and Mary Magdalene, with Christ at his death and Dismas' given appellation, *The Good Thief,* resonates throughout the history of the Church.

What do we know about Dismas?

The good thief Dismas is the first human being Christ canonized as a saint of the Church he founded upon earth, sealing it by taking him to Paradise the day they both died.

This is a singular event in the history of Christ's ministry on earth, a singular event in human history, and a singular event in the conversion of criminals, for there is no more powerful intercessionary saint than Saint Dismas.

His story should play a major role in prison ministry and a powerful source book for his story is *Life of The Good Thief* by Monsignor Gaume (2003), in which we find the following.

> When we consider all the circumstances of time and place, we cannot help repeating that the justice of the Good Thief, as well as all his other virtues, seems to us to have reached a perfection so great as to be unsurpassed, if not unrivalled, by that of any other Saint. None other, we may safely say, showed more heroic zeal for the glory of God, and the conversion of souls: more humility, more faith, more trust, more perfect love, at any given moment of his life, than did Dismas in the midst of the agonies of death.

It may not here be out of place, to insert the following eloquent passage, taken from a sermon of the Abbot Godfrey of Vendome: "Four great things were possessed by the thief, who confessed Christ upon the cross—wisdom, which by the light of faith made known to him the divinity of Christ, and, this, when all the disciples had left and abandoned Him; justice, which, through charity, made him rebuke the blasphemies of the other thief; holiness, which enabled him to pray to Christ with faith and love; and lastly, the reward, for he was given a share in the Redemption, according to the words of our Lord: 'This day shalt thou be with Me in Paradise." (pp. 127-128)

What are we to make of these signature events in the death of Christ accompanied by the two proto criminal saints?

I believe, with Monsignor Gaume, that:

Our Lord, throughout his life, and especially in the smallest details of his Sacred Passion, fulfilled every type and every prophecy. Whence in very truth he was able to say, when expiring upon the cross, "It is finished." (*Ibid* p. 71)

Dismas' life is a paradigm for the conversion of criminals; on the Egypt Road from the *Arabic Gospel of the Infancy,* how his essentially good heart recognized the Holy Family, and in his final moments, recognized God hanging beside him, God, the fount of the social teaching of the Church.

When we talk about the social teaching we are not talking about philosophical ramblings, new age meanderings, or occult ravings, but absolute truth revealed to us by the God-Man Christ, preserved for us by his Apostles, taught to us by the Fathers and Doctors of the Church, captured within the works of Peter and the universal *Catechisms* of Trent and Vatican II.

As we surely will, and often, encounter Modernism in our ministry, it is crucial to get our response right, as the Church has had it right since the beginning, as Modernism is nothing but the ancient heresy of Gnosticism— salvation by knowledge—in new language, but to know that you need to go to the source, you need to refresh yourself at the pool of clear water, the water of life.

Absolute truth resonates with your soul, and when you read the works of the greatest of all teachers, the Angelic Doctor St. Thomas Aquinas, the absolute truth rings out with stunning force.

Most teachers of the social teaching describe the 1891 encyclical *Rerum Novarum* (On Capital and Labor) by Pope Leo XIII as the beginning of the modern social teaching, but the teaching is all 'modern' because it is all eternal and the social teaching of Genesis is as crucial to our understanding of today as it was in the beginning.

One aspect of the modern interpretation of the social teaching—favored by liberation theologists and related liberal Catholics—is the preferential option for the materially poor.

This is a misreading of the teaching of the Church—as misread as the worldly tendency to think the materially rich are superior to the spiritually rich—for it is the spiritually poor who suffer most eternally. Christ revealed the truth of the spiritually rich and the materially rich to us in the parables of the widow's mite (Mark 12:41-44) and the rich young man (Mark 10: 17-31).

There have always been internal corruptions of the divine teaching and throughout the two thousand year history of the organized Catholic Church on earth, there have been, and will continue to be, many wayward, incompetent, misguided, and evil individuals among the laity and the priesthood, even stretching to the papacy.

In times within my memory the greatest disruption of the Church came around the time of Vatican II (1962-1965), when the entire Church seemed to wander ebulliently in the golden fields of temptation and dreams proffered by the world.

Communism and Marxist analysis drove a great degradation of the Latin American Church through Liberation Theology, spearheaded by the Jesuits—see

Jesuit Malachi Martin's book, *The Jesuits: The Society of Jesus and the Betrayal of the Roman Catholic Church*—which, through the choice of power over principle by the first Catholic president in America, led by the corruption of arguments protecting the life of the unborn and the virtual heresy of generations of Catholic politicians, see *The Politics of Abortion* by Alice Hendershott; all of which is undergirded by the changes emanating from the corrupted reading of the documents of Vatican II, see *Iota Unum: A Study of Changes in the Catholic Church in the XXth Century,* by Romano Amerio.

Upon this opening of the citadel to the serpent came the latest manifestation of the prince of this world's power to drive the Church to distraction, the sexual abuse crisis that engulfed—and still engulfs—the Church.

All this is the corruption from within attempting to destroy the Church, but that from without was more, much more.

The Roman emperors established precedence, as Crocker (2001) notes:

> What was crucially important about the persecutions that began under Nero and continued under Domitian was that they established the legal precedent that Christians could be singled out for punishment solely on the basis of their belief. (p. 16)

The decades of fire from the last century and beyond are within living memory.

In Mexico...Between November 11th 1931, and April 28th 1936, four hundred and eighty Catholic churches, schools, orphanages, and hospitals were closed by the Government or converted to other uses. They became cinemas, offices, garages, shops, libraries, and anything else one can imagine. The Mexican governments of the 1920's and 1930s were not content with nationalization. Under Mexico's socialist dictators, the Church suffered, in the words of Graham Greene, "the fiercest persecution of religion anywhere since the reign of Elizabeth." (*Ibid* p. 396)

The destruction of churches, the execution of priests, the seizure of all Church property, and the outlawing of the faith in Mexico proceeded with little international outcry. To liberal, or Protestant, eyes, the war waged by Mexican radicals against the Church was, after all, a Latin American issue. Turbulence was common in that part of the world, and undoubtedly modernization required that the illiberal, rapacious, corrupt, and backward Catholic Church be dismantled and the people freed from its superstitions. This attitude of Western, liberal, secular opinion, rooted in materialist assumptions, was something that Catholicism obviously did not share, and which allowed the faith to understand the truth at the heart of statist threats—like Communism and Nazism—sooner and more deeply than any other institution in the West; sooner certainly than Protestants, who, as Paul Johnson noted with regard to the German Protestant churches of the 1930s, "had no anti-state tradition...Since Luther's day they had always been in the service of the State, and indeed in many ways had come to see themselves as civil servants." Catholics, on the other hand, were regularly martyred by statist and communist regimes, perhaps most famously in the twentieth century in republican Spain.

There, in the 1930's, the sky was lit with the fire of burning churches; the soil bleached with the bones of the slaughtered faithful. For decades, politics in Spain had been bitterly divided between left and right, with each side occasionally claiming the government. Such exchanges of power did not lead to moderation, or stability, or an attitude of "better luck next time," but to hardening ideologies and extremism. On the left, anti-clericalism had alienated the center parties, as on the right it was accusations that the pro-Catholic, pro-monarchy, pro-military forces were edging into fascism. In 1936, with the country almost evenly divided, but the left claiming a narrow electoral victory, the arguments degenerated into blows. Increasing leftist disorders—from strikes to attacks on churches—were the justification for an attempted military coup. The coup was disorganized. Rather than suddenly seizing power, the country divided itself into warring factions. The military—the Nationalists—tried to shelter the Church, while the leftists—the Republicans—unleashed a blitzkrieg of anti-Catholic violence. Nearly seven thousand Catholic priests and religious were murdered—and most of these in the first months of the war, before the Nationalists could provide safe havens.

Nuns were raped, monks were shot, and priests were tortured and humiliated unless they repudiated their vows. Instead, the phrase came again as they went to their deaths: *Viva Cristo Rey* [Long live Christ the King]. But martyrdom was not for the clergy alone. Catholic persons and property were at the mercy of leftist mobs. The British historian Hugh Thomas wrote: "At no time in the history of Europe, or even perhaps of the world, had so passionate a hatred of religion and all its works been shown."

Maybe. But if Spanish radicals crucified the Church in a bout of extreme ferocity, it is equally true that the rapes, murders, and desecrations had been seen so many times before—in every major outbreak of anti-Catholic revolution—that it seems not only horrible, but tedious, to recapitulate them. Luther's partisans had done this, mocking the sacraments when they occupied Rome as soldiers of the Holy Roman Empire. The French Revolutionaries had done their best to ridicule the faith, destroy it by violence, and de-Christianize France by law, coercion, armed mobs, and the substitution of a secular creed. The Soviets were the most effective persecutors, having no mercy at all for religion—let alone a *foreign* religion.

Through all these and other persecutions, the Church never wavered, nor even showed fear. It placed an endless trust in its regenerative powers. Never would the gates of Hell prevail against it. (*Ibid* pp. 397-399)

The Prison Ministry

The *Catechism of the Catholic Church* teaches us about the missionary path, which the prison ministry surely is, a hard, yet, potentially, rewarding path.

852 *Missionary paths.* The Holy Spirit is the protagonist, "the principal agent of the whole of the Church's mission." It is he who leads the Church on her missionary paths. "This mission continues and, in the course of history, unfolds the mission of Christ, who was sent to evangelize the poor; so the Church, urged on by the Spirit of Christ, must walk the road Christ himself walked, a way of poverty and obedience, of service and self-sacrifice even to death, a death from which he emerged victorious by his resurrection." So it is that "the blood of martyrs is the seed of Christians."

853 On her pilgrimage, the Church has also experienced the "discrepancy existing between the message she proclaims and the human weakness of those to whom the Gospel has been entrusted." Only by taking the "way of penance and renewal," the "narrow way of the cross," can the People of God extend Christ's reign. For "just as Christ carried out the work of redemption in poverty and oppression, so the Church is called to follow the same path if she is to communicate the fruits of salvation to men."

854 By her very mission, "the Church . . . travels the same journey as all humanity and shares the same earthly lot with the world: she is to be a leaven and, as it were, the soul of human society in its renewal by Christ and transformation into the family of God." Missionary endeavor requires patience. It begins with the proclamation of the Gospel to peoples and groups who do not yet believe in Christ, continues with the establishment of Christian communities that are "a sign of God's presence in the world," and leads to the foundation of local churches. It must involve a process of inculturation if the Gospel is to take flesh in each people's culture. There will be times of defeat. "With regard to individuals, groups, and peoples it is only by degrees that [the Church] touches and penetrates them and so receives them into a fullness which is Catholic." (#852-854)

The Lampstand prison ministry—for the protection of the ministers, the prisoners, and ultimately the objective furtherance of the ministry—is based upon community, distance, books, and time.

The ministry is built upon a community of parishioners, providing distance teaching to prisoners about the social teaching of the Church complimented by her history through the suggested books, and taking all of the time necessary to ensure conversion begins to take hold.

This ministry will provide a path to conversion for prisoners upon release, and for those prisoners who will never be released— who are serving life without the possibility of parole and who have the prison status to pursue the way of the prison monk or spiritual warrior—a transformative prison conversion that can occur through their study of the teaching and history of the Church.

This prison conversion is an optional outcome which can ultimately lead to the further conversion of other prisoners.

Some preparative and logistical elements of prison ministry should include:

- Four reference books which Lampstand suggests would be very important for the ministry group to read and discuss before beginning outreach are **(1)** *Inside the Criminal Mind: Revised and Updated Edition.* Stanton E. Samenow. Ph.D. (2004) **(2)** Criminal *Justice and the Catholic Church.* Fr. Andrew Skotnicki, O.

Carm. (2008) **(3)** The two volume work of Fr. Rodger Charles, SJ, *Christian Social Witness and Teaching: The Catholic Tradition from Genesis to Centesimus Annus,* (1998) **(4)** H. W. Crocker III, *Triumph*: *The Power and the Glory of the Catholic Church, A 2,000 Year History*, (2001).

- Set up a Post Office Box for distance teaching.
- A minimum of four parishioners are needed to start a ministry community.
- Seek a retired law enforcement parishioner to become part of the ministry.
- Group reading and response of all letters to and from prisoners.
- Work with a maximum of four prisoners at a time, with each weekly meeting focused on one of them, or with each monthly meeting focused on each of them sequentially, and one letter a month minimum to each, with money (for stamps, paper and envelopes, books, commitment).
- At the prison you choose to work with, ask for an interview with the Catholic Chaplain and the appropriate correctional officer to determine the details of prisoners you are dealing with, what are the

details of their criminal history—and make sure you have access to the public court record involving their crime and subsequent sentencing.

The importance of the Catholic Chaplain can not be overstated, as the Pontifical Council for Justice & Peace (2004) notes.

> *[T]he activity that prison chaplains are called to undertake is important, not only in the specifically religious dimensions of this activity but also in defence of the dignity of those detained.* Unfortunately, the conditions under which prisoners serve their time do not always foster respect for their dignity; and often, prisons become places where new crimes are committed. Nonetheless, the environment of penal institutions offers a privileged forum for bearing witness once more to Christian concern for social issues: "I was...in prison and you came to me" (Mathew 25:35-36) (#403) (Italics in original)

In addition to a retired law enforcement professional, the parish prison ministry would be very fortunate to have a transformed criminal as a ministry member, one who meets the eight benchmarks of deep knowledge leadership:

- Ten years in the criminal world (includes prison) committing crimes for money
- Five years in a maximum security federal or state prison and not an informant, pedophile, or rapist
- Ten years out of prison, off parole, crime free, and helping the community
- Educated about Catholic social teaching
- Master's degree
- Leader of a community transformation apostolate
- Married
- Catholic

Having someone who has actually been there, walking in the criminal's penitential, transformative shoes is vital, and Topping (2011) notes the importance of like to like.

> An ancient Greek proverb ran, "like is known by like"; a modern equivalent might be "it takes one to know one." For the intellectual life this means that you must love first before you can learn. This condition of soul is demanded as much from the good novelist as from the good physicist, the good teacher as

much as the good police officer. Human nature, atoms, children and justice are all loved by those who serve them well. It is no different with God. In theology this likeness between subject and object has a technical term, "connaturality" (cf. John Paul II, *Veritas Splendor* #64). Unlike the modern reductionist view where the knowing subject can remain distant and aloof from his or her object, in the classical and Christian view, all learning, but especially theological enquiry, requires transformation. Winning intimacy with God is like winning any beloved: you must become worthy to share in his intimate and transformative presence. (p. 26)

Transformed criminals who meet these eight benchmarks will very likely feel a great compassion for criminals, and it is a compassion built upon a real understanding and sensitivity of the criminal/carceral world.

The depth of the criminal/carceral world's culture generally precludes the possibility of wide-spread conversion inside prison except for those certain prisoners with enough prison status able to transcend the prison culture without repercussions, and it is in the very process of conversion itself, in which the ministry seeks the resulting change repentance calls for, the metanoia, which Hardon (1999) describes:

It means a change of mind from unbelief to faith, and a change of heart from sin to the practice of virtue. As conversion, it is fundamental to the teaching of Christ, was the first thing demanded by Peter on Pentecost, and is considered essential to the pursuit of Christian perfection. (p. 349)

The demand of deep conversion, a real change of heart, is described by Barron (1998).

The English word "repent" has a moralizing overtone, suggesting at a change in behavior or action, whereas Jesus' term seems to be hinting at a change at a far more fundamental level of one's being. Jesus urges his listeners to change their way of knowing, their way of perceiving and grasping reality, their perspective, their mode of *seeing*. What Jesus implies is this: the new state of affairs has arrived, the divine and human have met, but the way you customarily see is going to blind you to this novelty. In the gnostic Gospel of Thomas, Jesus expresses the same concern: "The Kingdom of God is spread out on the earth, *but people do not see it.*" Minds, eyes, senses, perceptions—all have to be opened up, turned around, revitalized. *Metanoia,* soul transformation, is Jesus' first

49

recommendation. (Italics in original p. 4)

The lack of Peter's demand and Christ's primary recommendation in most prison ministries are why many, particularly non-Catholic ministries, are able to claim evangelical success in prison, for an actual and deeply internal change of life is not required. A mere expression of salvation is enough to bring the prisoner to the rolls of the saved, though saved in this scenario rarely equates with transformation.

In the evaluation of one of the largest religious prison ministries in the United States, involvement in the program actually increased recidivism—when evaluated appropriately—as noted by Fairhurst (2006) commenting on Mears, D. P., Roman, C. G., Wolff, A., & Buck, J., Faith-based efforts to improve prisoner reentry: Assessing the logic and evidence, *Journal of Criminal Justice*, 2006 August, Vol. 34 Iss. 4, (pp. 351-367).

> The fundamental flaw in all the studies: the absence of a clear, consistent operational definition of "faith-based." Is it, for example, nonprofit organizations with religious affiliations delivering secular services such as vocational and drug counseling—or is it individual faith volunteers conducting Bible classes with prisoners? Furthermore, where gains were

declared, it was unclear which practices or combinations of secular and religious components generated them.

Regardless of the definitions and measurements used and the manner in which findings were presented, the review found few studies that had generated data credible enough to justify public support—or outright rejection—of faith-based programming.

As an example, Mears cites the Prison Fellowship Ministries, founded by Charles Colson, the former Nixon aide who became a born-again Christian while imprisoned for his part in the Watergate scandal. Colson has touted the success of his ministries based on studies that show lower recidivism rates among participants. However, Mears noted that the studies focused only on inmates who completed the program, while comparing its recidivism rates to those of all participants—including dropouts—of selected secular programs.

In fact, if recidivism rates in Colson's programs were revised to include all participants, "graduates" or not, results would be worse than those for the comparison groups. Where successes might be construed to exist, it's unclear what to credit—the computer and life skills classes or its fundamentalist Christian doctrine. Where recidivism increases among its program participants, did faith-based programming play a part by leading some inmates to believe that ultimate responsibility for their actions lies with God, not them? Like arguments that faith-based programs decrease recidivism, this possibility remains to be demonstrated empirically. (n.p.)

What we see—with the force and vigor characteristic of the prison ministry efforts of the evangelical sects most deeply associated with prison ministry currently, is an urgency, a coercive pleading to act, now, and within this is an implied (and sometimes actually supplied) connection to outside resources and influences—is not characteristic of the Catholic conversion process, with its built-in year or so of study prior to being allowed to become baptized, for as Guardino (1956) reminds us.

Isn't this the real reason why money and power endanger the divine tidings, which remain so much stronger in weakness? (1 Cor. 1:25). The word made known by force does not bring Christ. Influence based on money and power does not bring God, for such things make void the means by which God himself entered the world. (p. 126)

Within this ministry cohort also, most efforts are primarily emotional, about which Humphreys (2011) writes.

> Our feelings are not the best indicators of our spiritual health, nor are they a reliable way to assess spiritual experiences. We should not mistake positive emotions for spiritual depth. Loud praising, singing, clapping and rousing shouts of *Amen* express emotion, but cannot replace the intimacy of quietly listening to God's voice within us. Feelings are transient, one giving way to another, and one day they can disappear and leave us by the wayside. It is only when the great highs of emotion recede that the roots of faith begin to deepen. (p. 23)

When I was studying the social teaching and history of the Church during the months of my conversion process, it very often felt like prayer as I read the encyclicals of Peter and studied the documents of Vatican II, quiet thoughtful prayer, of seeking, pondering, and finding.

Effective Catholic prison ministry is a quiet, thoughtful walk between horror and hope; always remaining conscious of the horrible acts those being ministered to have done and can still do, while remaining hopeful for a redeemed future.

A thoughtful reliance on presenting the history and the social teaching of the Catholic Church is optimal, as Mirus (2010) noted in a profile of Lampstand.

> This last point is extremely interesting, and it brings us back to questions about the larger social order. Lukenbill is saying, in effect, that the criminal mentality is based (more or less deliberately) on a skewed theory of how society works or ought to work. It is therefore hard to counter without a comprehensive and compelling theory of one's own. For David Lukenbill, Catholic social teaching provided that alternative theory, a consistent narrative of how society ought to work which can get inside even a criminal's head. (n.p)

What is so powerful about the evangelical power of the social teaching is, in addition to a depiction of "how society ought to work" is that—when studied in conjunction with the history of the Church—it reveals largely how the Church herself *has* worked over the 2,000 plus years of her existence on earth, an existence magnifying the divine power of love and an existence validating *walking the talk*, absolutely crucial to trump the criminal/carceral world narrative. Pope Benedict XVI (2006) writes.

1. "God is love, and he who abides in love abides in God, and God abides in him" (*1 Jn* 4:16). These words from the *First Letter of John* express with remarkable clarity the heart of the Christian faith: the Christian image of God and the resulting image of mankind and its destiny. In the same verse, Saint John also offers a kind of summary of the Christian life: "We have come to know and to believe in the love God has for us". (p.7)

That love calls on us to respond to others in the same spirit and while seeing Christ in all people is often rightfully at the heart of virtually all of the ministries of the Church, it should not be so in the prison ministry.

Here in this evil-soaked world, the actions of Christ we need remember are those of the exorcism of demons and remember that from the very model of penitential criminality proclaimed by Christ, Mary Magdalene, seven demons were cast out.

The ministry of teaching has exorcistic power and teaching the great social knowledge of the Church is the point of the sword for the prisoner, for it will be a field he enters willingly, as his search for hidden knowledge is eternally sated, calling him on to deeper exploration.

About the path of transformative learning, Schuyler (2004) notes:

55

- Small steps, within one's comfort zone, are the sole path toward transformational learning. This allows for sufficient assimilation and integration of the new learning so that it becomes a natural part of one's approach to life....
- "No limits assumed" is the only viable way to work toward transformation.
- Go where the problem isn't, not where it is, for the greatest learning. (p. 15)

What is wonderful in one way, but can be deceptive in another, is the great value the American public places on a virtuous life. We need only examine the aftermath of a public figure—whether in the Church or not—whose life appears to exemplify the highest American standards, when it is revealed that their private life is diametrically opposed to their public.

Within the value the public places on virtue, lies another weapon in the dismantling of the criminal/carceral world narrative—that all worldly life is, in its essence, criminal.

Criminals believe this, that the animating energy of worldly life is greed and lust and if criminal methods are necessary to satisfy these, most individuals in the world will use those methods.

However, the value the world places on the virtuous life lived completely can be used to demonstrate, ultimately, the shallow hold criminality really has.

Lampstand's work began with a focus on penitential criminals after they leave prison because, we—as prisoners and former prisoners—understand that virtually all prison conversions are a ruse, for it is only through freedom, whether freedom conferred by a high status inside prison or after release, that conversion is true.

Everything in prison—except what occurs between prisoners—is infected with the coercive nature of the prison, rendering conversion stories without the validation of after-prison life or the freedom of a natural life sentence, virtually meaningless.

The only strategy effectively rehabilitating criminals is one involving an inner change and the only narrative capable of creating that inner change is one based on verifiable truth, and it is the verifiable truth of the internal social teaching of the Church, wrapped within the external history of the Church, which provides a pathway to change.

Into the deep we must go, to rescue souls cast into the path of hell by their grasping of the baubles thrown about by the prince of this world, and the saving words are within a 2,000 year history of teaching, of goodness and struggling pilgrims against the world. The only true city on the hill is the one built by the divinity of Christ—founder and father of the Catholic Church.

Guiding us is Christ's establishment of the way of the prison ministry with his clear call to minister to the criminal, in prison and out. We see it magnificently manifested in the closeness he felt to St. Mary Magdalene, and the Golgotha canonization of St. Dismas, and his statements in response to the Pharisees who were murmuring against him for eating with tax collectors and sinners: "I have not come to call the righteous, but sinners to repentance." (Luke 5:32) For who are the greatest sinners if not the criminals wherein devils flourish and grow strong.

Criminals who make the journey from the criminal world to the communal with their honor intact, must make the rest of their life meaningful by harvesting the fruit of turning evil to good for other penitential criminals and the communal world they are now part of.

Know that the prison may be the greatest apostolate of all.

The prison first enters Western consciousness through Genesis and the story of Joseph sold by his brothers into slavery and ultimately becoming a prisoner, as found in Peters (1995).

> Joseph's prison was the "Great Prison," the *hnrt wr* at Thebes, present-day Luxor, whose existence is unrecorded before the period of the Middle Kingdom. [2050-1786 B.C.] (p. 9)

Skotnicki (2008) sees the contemporary prison emanating from the Catholic Church, as he wrote.

> My own conclusion is that the prison as we know it in the West originated in the penitential practice of the early church and in primitive monastic communities. With some reservations, I argue that it thus bears a meaning as valid and necessary as penance and monasticism themselves. Perhaps a more restrained way of phrasing it would be that since the contemporary prison is in many ways a Catholic innovation, whatever hope it may have as a locus and vehicle of criminal justice lies within the history we are about to survey. (p. 6)

Visiting those in prison is given us as a work of corporal mercy by Christ, when he teaches us: "...I was in prison and you came to me." (Matthew 25: 36)

The *Catechism* teaches us about the works of mercy.

> The *works of mercy* are charitable actions by which we come to the aid of our neighbor in his spiritual and bodily necessities. Instructing, advising, consoling, comforting are spiritual works of mercy, as are forgiving and bearing wrongs patiently. The corporal works of mercy

consist especially in feeding the hungry, sheltering the homeless, clothing the naked, visiting the sick and imprisoned, and burying the dead. (#2447)

With these four elements in mind: the prison as an ancient institution, the prison in the modern West as Catholic inspired, prison visits as works of mercy, and works of mercy as how we aid one another; the Lampstand prison ministry is a spiritual work of mercy directed to prisoners in maximum security prisons, for the purpose of evangelization and the development of transformative criminal/carceral leadership who will then be able to help other prisoners.

Soon after I began Lampstand I had an opportunity to go into a local prison to work with a program that was generating some publicity for its work and I soon realized it was a protective custody wing of the prison, housing those prisoners—informants, pedophiles, serial rapists—who needed protection from the other prisoners.

As the work of the Lampstand Foundation is directed towards developing leaders among the criminal/carceral world whose status ensures the widest respect from other prisoners/criminals they could be bringing to the Church, work within protective custody prisons was not work providing that level of optimization.

Fortunately, the population in maximum security prisons is substantial.

At the end of 2010, according to the Bureau of Justice Statistics (2011) there were 1,518,104 prisoners in federal and state prisons. (p. 3)

The population in maximum security prisons, noted by Useem & Piehl (2008) hovers around 40% of the total—including super-maximum security prisons which accounts for 1-2%.

> In 1974, about 44% of the inmates in state confinement facilities were housed in maximum security prisons; by 2000, this percentage declined to about 38%. (p. 105)

The reason to focus on the prisoners in maximum security prisons is because they are able, if converted, to lead others to conversion that can hold, due to their influential status in the criminal/carceral world. Christ calls us to extend our evangelical reach to the greatest sinners whose conversion creates the greatest joy in heaven, as revealed in the mystery of the prodigal son and the compassion he felt for the two proto criminal saints, Mary Magdalene and Dismas, the penitential criminals at the point and the root of the cross.

Maximum security prisoners are largely professional criminals—those who commit crimes for money and as a career—with a strong commitment to the carceral/criminal world, and it is in the roots of that commitment that the possibility of a commitment to conversion lays.

Professional criminals—those who commit crimes for money—according to the Bureau of Justice Statistics (2010), have the highest rearrest rates.

> Released prisoners with the highest rearrest rates were robbers (70.2%), burglars (74.0%), larcenists (74.6%), motor vehicle thieves (78.8%), those in prison for possessing or selling stolen property (77.4%), and those in prison for possessing, using, or selling illegal weapons (70.2%). (n.p.)

Maximum security prisoners in the general population are not informants or pedophiles—who will not long survive except in protective custody. The evil of the acts of the pedophile and informant (informant being someone who, after being apprehended, betrays those he committed crimes with) is described in Christ's own words, respectively.

> Matthew 18:6 - "Whoever causes one of these little ones who believe in me to sin, it would be better for him to have a great millstone hung around his neck and to be drowned in the depths of the sea."

> Matthew 26:24 - "The Son of Man indeed goes, as it is written of him, but

woe to that man by whom the Son of Man is betrayed. It would be better for that man if he had never been born."

Pope Benedict XVI (2010) comments on Judas:

Judas is neither a master of evil nor the figure of a demonical power of darkness but rather a sycophant who bows down before the anonymous power of changing moods and current fashion. But it is precisely this anonymous power that crucified Jesus, for it was anonymous voices that cried, 'Away with him! Crucify him!' (p. 73)

The seminal betrayal by Judas was defined by Christ, "Judas, Would you betray the Son of man with a kiss?" (Luke 22:48)

Why was the betrayal by Judas the epitome, the archetype of betrayal? Is it because it is only from one who is known and loved that a kiss is trustingly received and ultimately, betrayal can at times follow.

The *Oxford Dictionary* (1993) defines Judas as: "A person who treacherously betrays another under the semblance of friendship; a traitor or betrayer of the worst kind." (p. 1458)

It is this turning away by the betrayer, from who they loved, toward their own self-interest of survival—away from sacrificing self on the altar of brotherhood and friendship—away from solidarity to selfishness.

Betrayers, pedophiles, and rapists are virtually never willing to change and it is this obstinacy, as St. Thomas Aquinas (1948) teaches us, wherein even God's mercy is conditional.

> God, for His own part, has mercy on all. Since, however, His mercy is ruled by the order of His wisdom, the result is that it does not reach to certain people who render themselves unworthy of that mercy, as do the demons and the damned who are obstinate in wickedness. And yet we may say that even in them His mercy finds a place, in so far as they are punished less than they deserve condignly, but not that they are entirely delivered from punishment. (*Summa*, Q. 99 Art. 2, Reply Obj. 1.)

The professional criminal's immersion within the carceral/criminal world is spurred by his search for freedom, money, and power, which, from his perspective, is an honorable path—in itself and without accepting restrictions—as defined by the way of the world.

Professional criminals occupy the upper echelon within carceral/criminal culture and are most apt to respond to an intellectual ministry approach based on the social teaching of the Church and will, once converted, also share it with others—who will listen to them.

The ministry objective is to present the truths of the faith in the catechetical way to increase the potential for truth's reception, while deflecting the potential manipulative abuse of a personal relationship, because, in Gehenna, as Hahn (2009) wrote: "as the place where the rebels against the Lord will be strewn" (p. 305), it is Catholic truth which will free, not a relationship always being tested.

The only relationship which will break the hardness of the evil in prison is the personal one with Christ, and the intellectual one with the *words* of Peter and the saints.

The ideal prison ministry as a spiritual work of mercy, metaphorically, is like the Latin Mass where the ministers and the prisoners will both be facing Christ, not each other.

Traditional prison ministry practiced as a corporal work of mercy is from a simpler time, when many prisoners were first-time felons and often eagerly penitential. As the carceral/criminal world has deepened over the past several decades in America, only the most hardened go to prison. Within the maximum security prison the criminal culture is mandated—there are no bystanders—penance is weakness and weakness is surrender or death.

The greatest danger in prison ministry as a spiritual work of mercy—especially if you attempt it as an individual—is that you will very possibly be used for the prisoner's purpose rather than your purpose of helping bring him to conversion. Working in a group reduces the chance of this occurring.

A primal description of the prince of the criminal world—father of lies—is earned for an eternal method, not an occasional tool, for he lies always and eternally, it is a way of being and the professional criminal embraces the way of the world.

The imprisoned professional criminal is often an adept weaver of word magic schooled in the charm and glamour of criminal/carceral world darkness, and can usually induce the traditional evangelist—sometimes susceptible to that charm and glamour—to accept his claim of salvation. In the acceptance of a false salvation, the evangelist can become victim rather than witness.

In these dangerous fields, the evangelist once removed and armed with a deep understanding of the social teaching of the Church, will be engaging the prisoner intellectually and will reap a bounty of much deeper root.

The Lampstand apostolate focuses on professional criminals because this is the cohort I know and respect and for many years was part of, in prison and out.

Other prison ministries are apostolates who lump all criminals and prisoners into one cohort, not realizing how limiting this approach renders their work. It is impossible to respect an effort which does not understand the reality of the most basic criminal/carceral world typology and it will be very difficult for the criminal/prisoner to connect with an effort they do not respect.

A dilutive concept—in concert with the abolition of capital punishment currently enjoying some favor among many in the Church—impeding effective prison ministry in maximum security prisons, is restorative justice.

Abolishing capital punishment and replacing the traditionally straightforward Catholic teaching about crime and punishment with the restorative justice trend—strongly connected to the liberation theology trend—is seductive to many, but it is the constancy and clarity of Catholic teaching that has protected our faith from the gates of hell, not succumbing to trendy seductions.

Restorative justice grew out of the pacifistic perspective of some non-Catholic faith traditions—where no defense is mounted against evil as a signifier of Christian love—which is alien to a Catholic economy which historically confronts evil at every turn.

Weigel (1987) notes the thought of St. Augustine concerning pacifism.

> Augustine was no militarist; there is no glorification of war in *The City of God*, and Augustine held in contempt those who saw conquest as a noble aspiration (Alaric's sack of Rome in 410 surely had an effect here). But Augustine broke decisively with the pacifism and antimilitarism of earlier Church fathers

such as Tertullian, Origen, and Lactantius. In this fallen world, war was inevitable. Like the authority of the state, war exists in God's providential plan as an instrument for punishment, so that a minimum of justice—that is, order—may be maintained. Just as the damned are part of God's plan for the heavenly City, so war could be a part of peace. On this view, pacifism was a concession to evil and injustice. (p. 29)

Many translate Jesus' surrender to crucifixion as evidence of his pacifism— *allowing* evil its way—but it was surrender to his earthly mission of redemption, the eternal victory *over* evil that guided him.

Beirne & Messerschmidt (2011) describe restorative justice as seen from a socio/Marxist perspective.

CRITICAL HUMANIST CRIMINOLOGIES
Under the umbrella of critical criminology are several perspectives that focus on humanizing the institutions of criminal justice. (p. 220)

A combination of diversity in perspective and leftist politics also lies at the heart of several other humanist tendencies in critical criminology. Among these are abolitionism, anarchism and restorative justice....

Restorative justice.

"Reintegrative" or "constructive" shaming is the central tactical mechanism in the movement of **restorative justice**, which began in New Zealand and Australia and which is based on conferencing with victims and offenders. During conferences offenders are confronted by their victims and by their victims' friends and families in an effort to help them understand the harm they have caused others through their wrongful actions or omissions. At the same time, victims are encouraged not to see offenders as vile and fixed objects of punitiveness but to understand them as existing somewhere between authentic beings and beings with damaged identities who likely did what they did because of sociological and psychological circumstances over which they had little or no control. (*Ibid* pp. 222-223)

While we can appreciate the enhanced discussion the concept of restorative justice has brought to the criminal justice dialogue, its utility with professional criminals who have served time in maximum security prisons and are the dominant group defining and shaping criminal/carceral world culture, is much too limited, primarily because they understand—expressed often and clearly when among themselves—what is also at the heart of Catholic social teaching; that crime is primarily the result of individual choice, not "sociological and psychological circumstances".

With professional criminals, the salvific tool with the greatest potency is the classical Catholic teaching of punishment, penance, and redemption.

In a seminal article Fr. Andrew Skotnicki (2006) examines restorative justice from a Catholic perspective.

> Restoration is a principal component of justice; but it is not the only component. Justice also requires punishment. The schema for restoration suggested by contemporary philosophers and criminologists would require a thicker description of the nature and meaning of criminal offences, as well as a more substantial role for the state as representative of the body politic...
>
> The answer is that justice demands both punishment and re-integration. The offence against God's commandments, against the harmony of the universe and the sanctity of creation must be addressed. (pp. 192-193)

Congruent with liberation theology and the consistent ethic of life—primal positions of liberal Catholics—restorative justice tends to relativize Catholic social teaching away from the Church's traditional essence, so well thought out by St. Thomas Aquinas and other great Catholic thinkers, which sees the Church as a sign of contradiction to the normative vision of seeking worldly popularity and influence, as Mirus (2010) notes.

> The inroads of Modernism, the treason of the intellectuals in colleges and universities, the seduction of many traditional religious orders, and the desire of bishops to avoid conflict (and be perceived as players) have all led to a public image for the Church as something of a fiddler—fiddling, so to speak, while Rome burns. (n.p)

Restorative justice animates an idea shared by liberal Catholics, that Church practice should be decided democratically, as Skotnicki (2006) notes:

> Unlike contemporary courtroom dynamics that are generally characterized by a decidedly impersonal tug of war between rival attorneys, with plaintiff and defendant relegated to secondary and isolated roles, restorative justice is a process whereby all the parties with a stake in a particular offence come together to resolve collectively how to deal with the

aftermath of the offence and its implications for the future. (p. 188)

Traditional Catholic teaching concerning crime and justice is based upon revelation in scripture, traditional practice, and magisterial teaching from the great Catholic thinkers.

The professional criminal realizes this diversion by restorative justice into, essentially, the will of the moment, particularly as he studies Catholic social teaching and history and it will be the consistent linkage with the roots of that teaching to Church history that will call him to embrace Catholicism today.

Understanding the power of interior reflection provided by the prison is a compelling factor in effective prison ministry. It is remarked on by Pearce (1999) in his biography of Solzhenitsyn—though the strengthening of the American prisoner's interiority is usually in the opposite direction—its power is evident nonetheless.

> Solzhenitsyn was clearly concerned never to lose sight of the truths he had learned in the camps, never to allow the comforts of life to corrupt him from the purity of the vision he believed he had acquired there. It was precisely 'the highest, noblest impulses of the soul that he felt he had discovered in prison and precisely those impulses that he

was determined the material pleasures of life should not obscure. (p. 140)

Unless prison ministers come to some understanding of the forging power—the deep strengthening of the will of those who, rather than being cowed, become more deeply unbowed and resolute as a result of the prison experience—and the refining of the criminal world culture through the carceral experience, it will be impossible to appreciate the level of resistance to eternal truth by that of worldly truth animating the carceral/criminal world.

While true conversion is rare in prison, especially on the mainline of a maximum security facility, the introduction of the intellectual concepts and history of the social teaching of the Church in conjunction with its institutional history in the world, is a presentation of truth capable of trumping the criminal/carceral world truth the criminal relies on and it may remain with him long enough to develop enough traction to become of some direction upon his release.

The social teaching presented in conjunction with Church history can be found in many books but I would recommend the two volume work of Rodger Charles SJ, (1998) *Christian Social Witness and Teaching: The Catholic Tradition from Genesis to Centesimus Annus*; and by H. W. Crocker III, (2001) *Triumph: The Power and the Glory of the Catholic Church, A 2,000 Year History*, as works to place in the hands of prisoners after the first ministry contact.

There are simpler, introductory books to Charles's teaching: *An Introduction to Catholic Social Teaching* and *An Introduction to Catholic Social Teaching: Study Guide*—as the two volumes recommended are graduate level works—but please resist the temptation to use them and go for the fullest expression of his work, remembering that the prisoner has huge blocks of time available to him in which to enter into the deepest study and it will be the effort required, amplified by the ministry correspondence, which will open the prisoner's mind to the truths of the Church.

The 2,000+ year history of the Church on the earth, connected with the constancy of its social teaching through the worldly battlefields threatening it, is a true story of triumph, courage, honor, and truths held hard, that can resonate with the professional criminal, whose life is lived more than may be evident, by those same qualities, though clearly corrupted.

In the process of presenting the history of the Church, stories from the lives of the saints can be especially instructive, particularly from the great criminal saints, one of which was the criminal who became Peter, who I wrote about in my book *Carceral World, Communal City*.

96) From the very beginning, criminals played a major role in the Church—the good thief Dismas being an early example—and another was the transformed criminal who became pope, St. Callistus (died 222). His experience-based decree selection caused a severe political break in the Church, but restored its heart of mercy and redemption, when he decreed forgiveness for major sinners after confession and penance, against the wishes of many early Christians. As Craughwell (2006) explains:

> Callistus' brief five-year reign was marked by the virtue he had come to appreciate above all others. He decreed that Christians who had committed fornication or adultery, even Christians who had fallen into heresy, could be restored to full Communion with the Catholic Church once they had confessed their sins and done penance. Pope Callistus' ruling split the Church between orthodox Catholics who understood that the Church was in the forgiveness business, and more rigid Catholics who felt that certain sins were unforgivable. The leader of the inflexible faction was Hippolytus, a Roman priest and theologian,

who knew about Callistus' shameful past and despised him for it. An angry, vindictive man, Hippolytus taught that any Christian who committed even a single mortal sin ought to be driven out of the Church and never permitted to return, no matter how sincerely he or she might repent. (Craughwell, T. J. (2006). *Saints behaving badly: The cutthroats, crooks, trollops, con men, and devil-worshippers who became saints.* New York: Doubleday. p. 15)

This inflexibility and strict adherence to the language of the Church's law rather than the spirit of it marks some brief moments in the history of the Church, as of all institutions, but none walks the talk as does the Church.

97) Hippolytus, the leader of those who attacked Callistus throughout his papacy was the anti-pope who came back to the Church, eventually becoming one of her fathers.

Hippolytus attacked Callistus with venom, and what struck me reading about his attacks and the ferocity with which they were raised, considering the great admiration most Catholics felt for Callistus, leads to the conclusion that perhaps what most troubled Hippolytus was that Callistus, a common criminal, was getting the honor he felt he, Hippolytus, deserved.

Callistus, as a redeemed criminal, understood better than most that redemption was always possible and Christ's message was, if it was anything, that all could be forgiven.

However, as Pope Callistus allowed many who had committed major sins to return, after proper penance, to the fold of the Church, Hippolytus and his supporters were enraged, feeling even the committing of one major sin precluded future involvement with the Church.

98) The powerful denouement to this wonderful story of two men—one pope and one anti-pope—in the early days of the Church; was that upon being imprisoned for claiming himself as pope in reaction to the acts of Pope Callistus, Hippolytus later redeemed himself, primarily as a result of the same sort of imprisonment once suffered by Callistus, and the knowledge gained from his suffering there.

As Foley & McCloskey (2003) note:

> Hippolytus was a strong defender of orthodoxy, and admitted his excesses by his humble reconciliation. He was not a formal heretic, but an overzealous disciplinarian. What he could not learn in his prime as a reformed and purist, he learned in the pain and desolation of imprisonment. (Foley, L. & McCloskey, P. (2003). *Saint of the day: Lives lessons and feasts*. Cincinnati; St. Anthony Messenger Press. p. 204)

Callistus, the prodigal son who became pope, fulfilled the inner lesson of the parable noted by Pope Benedict XVI (2007):

> The parable [of the prodigal son] breaks off here; it tells us nothing about the older brother's reaction. Nor can it, because at this point the parable immediately passes over into reality. Jesus is using these words of the father to speak to the heart of the murmuring Pharisees and scribes who have

grown indignant at his goodness to sinners. (Pope Benedict XVI. (2007). *Jesus of Nazareth: From the baptism in the Jordon to the Transfiguration.* New York: Doubleday. p. 209)

Callistus spoke to the heart of the Pharisees of his time with his goodness and forgiveness of sinners they would not forgive. (pp. 87-90)

The history of Callistus is a powerful story centered on the impact that time in prison can have and the heights to which a penitential criminal may climb.

A former prison minister, the Catholic priest Rev. Thomas J. Euteneuer (2010) writes:

For many years I was involved in prison ministry...

Ultimately, these environments, full of criminals, are also seedbeds for the works of the Evil One and therefore are in dire need of Christian ministry. The idea that a person goes to prison to become "reformed" is an absurdity. Oftentimes they become confirmed in their criminal ways.

I would ask ... anyone in prison ministry, to be of good cheer, fully confident that your work is blessed by

God because it is a work that Christ explicitly asked His Church to carry out. If the "official" Church does not pay proper attention to this work of the Gospel, then those in authority will be held accountable before the Judgment Seat of God. Ours, however, is not to agonize over what others are not doing, but to do what we are supposed to do with greater fervor, asking God to sanctify us in the process. (n.p.)

It is crucial to remember that the criminal—not society, capitalism, or the criminal justice system—is the problem.

Some Catholics who are attracted to prison ministry believe, due to the myths of Hollywood or Marxism shrouded within Liberation Theology, that the good guys are the criminals and the police, district attorneys, prison guards, and legislators who support stringent criminal sanctions, are the bad guys.

This stance does everyone a disservice—in particular the penitential criminal—who may find little reason for proper expiation within a culture defining criminality as somehow admirable.

Professional criminals understand that their criminality is only admirable in the context of the criminal/carceral world culture and if the ministry does not understand this, it will have little real resonance.

Also remember that regardless of the moral evil done by many Catholic bishops, priests, and laity—which will be thrown back at you during your ministry—the work of the Church on earth is magnificently good, strong, and true.

It will be your deep understanding of this history and the underlying social teaching, strengthened by your personal relationship with God that will eventually prove most valuable in your spiritual work of mercy with prisoners.

The sexual abuse in the Catholic Church over the past several decades has deeply hurt the Church, as Bower (2011) writes:

> When the public realized that the problem of clerical sex abuse was indeed pandemic, not merely limited to metropolises such as Boston and Los Angeles, Catholicism *as a religion* lost most of its credibility in the eyes of the world. In the current era of open (and often quite merited) hostility toward the Church as an institution, combined with the blatant hypocrisy of far too many of her administrators, no well-meaning bit of doctrine or apologetics will have quite the same punch when squared with the fact that Holy Mother Church has effectively destroyed her integrity—some might say for good. (p. 45)

Regardless, the only possible response is an aggressive one, and with sexual abuse, bringing up the past struggles the Church has had with this issue—prior to the golden age of Christendom—can serve as a reminder of the eternal influence of evil upon the hearts of men and the power of reform.

The sexual abuse horrors of the past several years within the Church, well documented in many books, reports and news stories, is best compiled in these five books: *Goodbye Good Men: How Liberals Brought Corruption into the Catholic Church,* by Michael S. Rose (2002), *The Rite of Sodomy: Homosexuality and the Roman Catholic Church,* by Randy Engel (2006), *The Faithful Departed: The Collapse of Boston's Catholic Culture,* by Philip F. Lawler (2008), *Sacrilege: Sexual Abuse in the Catholic Church,* by Leon J. Podles, and *After Asceticism: Sex, Prayer and Deviant Priests,* by the Linacre Institute (2006).

Within Randy Engel's magisterial book is a description of the work of Saint Peter Damian (1007-1072) born in Ravenna, Italy who became a physician and later, one of the great reformers of the Church.

He wrote Letter 31, *The Book of Gomorrah,* to Pope Leo IX, as Engel (2006) notes:

> ...in 1049 AD, which contains the most extensive treatment and condemnation by any Church Father of clerical pederasty and homosexual practices. (p. 48)

The Church has always been forced to deal with evil, indeed, that is one of her major missions, and her travails today are not new, nor shall they be the last, for on earth she is the Church Militant, which Hardon (1999) describes.

> The Church on earth, still struggling with sin, and temptation, and therefore engaged in warfare (Latin, *militia*) with the world, the flesh, and the devil. (p. 105)

Priests, even as well armed as they are with the tools of spiritual warfare, if working alone and without special training, will generally have difficulty evangelizing criminals as they tend to use God-talk, when the most effective method will be thought-talk, the social thought of the Church, revealing the historical practice and ideals of the human institution herself, for it is through the world that the criminal, caught deeply in the ways of the world, can come to eternity.

God-talk is what the criminal will eventually come to, on his own and quietly, within the interiority of his soul.

The emptiness of so much God-talk—associated most glaringly with the Protestant sects—repels rather than attracts the worldly-wise criminal. Approaching the criminal from a historical, doctrinal, intellectual plane, showing the institutional Church *walking the talk*, however, will attract his attention.

Prison chaplains rarely use the teachings of their religion for helping prisoners, as Mears, Roman, Wolff, & Buck (2006) note.

> ...their study of prison chaplains which found that 40 percent "did not select religion as the best method of treatment" and instead "feel that secular methods are better suited to bring about inmate change." (p. 353)

An important part of converting criminals through the social teaching is showing how that teaching—used by the institutional Church—impacted history. One of the clearest examples from recent history is the role Peter played in the defeat of communism, as noted by Weigel (2010).

> The notion that John Paul II played a pivotal role in the collapse of European communism was largely missed during and immediately after the Revolution of 1989 and the demise of the Soviet Union...

> Twenty-five years later, the true picture was coming into sharper focus. John Lewis Gaddis of Yale, America's premier historian of the Cold War...was unambiguous in his judgement on the

matter: "When John Paul II kissed the ground at the Warsaw airport on June 2, 1979, he began the process by which communism in Poland—and ultimately everywhere—would come to an end." Gaddis was not, of course, suggesting that John Paul was alone in bringing communism to its knees; rather, John Paul II was one of a number of leaders with the insight and courage to see a new situation and seize the opportunities inherent in it. (pp. 184-185)

God-talk tends to be connected to the individual delivering it, while the social teaching connects conversion to the institutional Church and Peter.

Individual God-talk sounds the same to the uber-worldly criminal, whether from Protestants or Catholics, while the history and social teaching of the Church—that reaches back to Genesis—can only come from the Catholic Church founded by Christ on the shoulders of Peter.

Prisoners in maximum security prisons are above all, pure realists—there are few things in life more real than a maximum security prison—and they *know* the nature of true justice, and it will only be from a full portrayal of the truth of the Catholic Church regarding justice, punishment, and reformation that true conversion will occur.

My memories of 12 years talking with my fellow prisoners, inclusive of my own familial history, is that we tend to view—with some pride—our personal history, even if it is horrific, as a necessary hardening for the world ahead.

Like another generation's story of trudging through five miles of waist high snow to school, proudly told, is the criminal/carceral cultural story of family violence, poverty, and personal suffering; though, if need be for social favor, we are always able to portray it according to the victim narrative many non-criminals hope to hear from us.

While speaking of God's love for us—God-talk—is *truly* speaking of the axis of the world and the divine ground upon which our lives on earth are lived, yet it can negate conversion; whereas the speaking of knightly power and chivalry and their greatest flowering in the Catholic warrior orders, noted by Seward (2000), *can* resonate the chord of conversion within the professional criminal's heart.

> The knight brethren of the military orders were noblemen vowed to poverty, chastity and obedience, living a monastic life in convents which were at the same time barracks, waging war on the enemies of the Cross. In their chapels one saw monks reciting the Office, but outside they were soldiers in uniform. The three great orders were the Templars, Hospitallers (Knights of

Malta) and Teutonic Knights, though Santiago and Calatrava were no less formidable. Most of them emerged during the twelfth century to provide the Church with storm-troopers for the Crusades. They were the first properly disciplined and officered troops in the West since Roman times. (p. 3)

That history of seeking justice through war is still at the heart of the Church in her teaching around abortion, just war, and capital punishment—all connected to protecting the innocent—and learning of it will deepen the criminal's search through the teaching and history of the Church.

These are stories that will truly excite the heart, mind, and spirit of the criminal, living a life within the daily threat of battle to the death in prison and needing strong internal resources to combat, survive, and for some, grow deeper spiritually.

Being able to provide daily mass within the prison will sacramentally sharpen the saintly path that some criminals serving natural life will begin to choose, as the *Catechism* teaches.

1070 In the New Testament the word "liturgy" refers not only to the celebration of divine worship but also to the proclamation of the Gospel and to active charity. In all of these situations it is a question of the service of God and neighbor. In a liturgical celebration the Church is servant in the image of her Lord, the one "*leitourgos*"; she shares in Christ's priesthood (worship), which is both prophetic (proclamation) and kingly (service of charity):

> The liturgy then is rightly seen as an exercise of the priestly office of Jesus Christ. It involves the presentation of man's sanctification under the guise of signs perceptible by the senses and its accomplishment in ways appropriate to each of these signs. In it full public worship is performed by the Mystical Body of Jesus Christ, that is, by the Head and his members. From this it follows that every liturgical celebration, because it is an action of Christ the priest and of his Body which is the Church, is a sacred action surpassing all others. No other action of the Church can equal its efficacy by the same title and to the same degree. (#1070)

The importance of having a dedicated Catholic Chaplaincy—staffed by a priest— in the prison cannot be overstated, and it is hoped that as the Church comes more to the realization of the great mission fields lying barren within the nation's maximum security prisons, and as the ranks of reformed Catholic prisoners reach out to the institutional Church for help in their prison apostolates, the Church will realize the paramount importance of developing specially trained priests to serve as prison chaplains.

During the crucifixion and resurrection of Our Lord, penitential criminals played central roles—St. Mary of Magdalene and St. Dismas—and it is because of these penitential criminal saints, in their names, and in the name of Our Lord who showed us the way, that we need to do all we can to ensure prisoners have full access to a Catholic priest.

Once the ministry team has been established, the prison has been selected, and work with the Catholic Chaplin at the prison has begun to develop relations with Catholic prisoners the chaplain feels may be most receptive to the intellectual work of learning about the social teaching and the history of the Church, the actual process can be developed.

Use the aforementioned works by Charles and Crocker in a structured process of mutual reading with the prisoners, amplified through letters, interaction through occasional visits with the prisoner, meetings with prison administrators and the Catholic priest, all buttressed by prayer.

Due to the differences in various regions of the country and within different prisons around visiting with and writing to prisoners, it is necessary to develop the specific logistics of contact and teaching based on those regional and specific prison factors, as well as the parish individuals involved in the ministry.

Though the heart of the ministry will remain the same, the particular methods of interaction will be different, depending on parish/prison differences.

Hierarchy of Evil

We begin our exploration of evil as perceived within the criminal/carceral world—vital to understand as a prequel to an effective prison ministry—by examining the criminal world perspective on the ground of evil's opposite, love.

Within the criminal/carceral world, love finds small consolation, for the harder edges of greed, lust, and power tend to cut it out.

The criminal/carceral world is intelligible once you discover the key, which is satanic thought, where the only human reality is self interest and love does not exist, only selfish drives to satisfy selfish desire.

It is as Lewis (2001)—recording the letters the devil Uncle Screwtape wrote to his devil nephew Wormwood—describes it.

> All His [God] talk about Love must be a disguise for something else—He must have some *real* motive for creating them and taking so much trouble about them. The reason one comes to talk as if He really had this impossible Love is our utter failure to find out that real motive. What does He stand to make out of them? That is the insoluble question. I do not see that it can do any harm to tell you that this very problem

was a chief cause of Our Father's [Satan] quarrel with the Enemy. When the creation of man was first mooted and when, even at that stage, the Enemy freely confessed that He foresaw a certain episode about a cross, Our Father very naturally sought an interview and asked for an explanation. The Enemy gave no reply except to produce the cock-and-bull story about disinterested love which He has been circulating ever since. This Our Father naturally could not accept. He implored the Enemy to lay His cards on the table, and gave Him every opportunity. He admitted that he felt a real anxiety to know the secret; the Enemy replied 'I wish with all my heart that you did.' It was, I imagine, at this stage in the interview that Our Father's disgust at such an unprovoked lack of confidence caused him to remove himself an infinite distance from the Presence with a suddenness which has given rise to the ridiculous Enemy story that he was forcibly thrown out of Heaven. Since then, we have begun to see why our Oppressor was so secretive. His throne depends upon the secret. Members of His faction have frequently admitted that if ever we came to understand what He means by love, the war would be over and we should re-enter Heaven. And there lies the great task. We know that He cannot really love: nobody can: it doesn't make sense. If we could only find out what He is *really* up to! (pp. 100-101)

Beginning from that place where love cannot exist, where its expressions are merely means to an end, we can examine the hierarchy of evil within the criminal/carceral world.

Professional criminals occupy the upper echelons within prison; informants, rapists and pedophiles the lower. The hierarchy is inverted as those on the lower are considered most evil and those on the upper least evil. For pastoral work related to the rehabilitation or conversion of criminals, this hierarchy plays a crucial role.

The work of my apostolate to help reform professional criminals through exposure to the history and social teaching of the Catholic Church, is only as effective as is my love for the professional criminal—those who commit crimes for money and are not informants, pedophiles, or rapists. That love is built on knowledge of the criminal world which I absorbed through twenty years as a criminal, with twelve years spent in maximum security state and federal prisons.

The love I have for criminals continues today, though it has been decades since I was in prison or living as a criminal among criminals, and it manifests itself in the pleasure and joyful anticipation I still feel when I have an opportunity to venture into a maximum security prison to speak with prisoners.

This love for the men and women professional criminals I came to know in the criminal/carceral world is built upon shared experiences and many shared perspectives of the world.

This love has grown as a result of my active immersion in Catholicism, begun during the months prior to entering the Rite of Christian Initiation for Adults, and deepened since my baptism and the founding of the apostolate.

I am not the person I once was. I am not the criminal I once was, yet I retain a deep respect and quiet love for the cultural artifacts of the criminal/carceral world and the moral principles that have marked criminals since the criminal Dismas received canonization hanging at Christ's side on Golgotha.

Love based on knowledge of the criminal/carceral world is central to an effective prison ministry, as it is central to all Catholic evangelism, noted by Adam (1937).

> An altitude of mere neutrality, or a cold realism is of no use here. Or, rather, only the man who himself lives in the Catholic life-stream, who in his own daily life feels the forces which pulsate through the vast body of Catholicism and make it what it is: only he can know the full meaning and complete reality of it. Just as the loving child alone can truly know the character of its beloved mother, and just as the deepest

elements of that character, the tenderness and intimacies of her maternal love, cannot be demonstrated by argument but only learnt by experience, just so only the believing and loving Catholic can see into the heart of Catholicism, and feeling, living, experiencing, discover with that "spirit de finesse" of which Pascal speaks, that is, with the comprehensive intuition of his innermost soul, the secret forces and fundamental motive powers of its being. (pp. 4-5)

One of the most poetic descriptions of love for criminals is from the criminal and author Jean Genet (1964), writing about his criminal life in France.

Convicts' garb is striped pink and white. Though it was at my heart's bidding that I chose the universe wherein I delight, I at least have the power of finding therein the many meanings I wish to find: *there is a close relationship between flowers and convicts*. The fragility and delicacy of the former are of the same nature as the brutal insensitivity of the latter. Should I have to portray a convict—or a criminal—I shall so bedeck him with flowers that, as he disappears beneath them, he will himself become a flower, a gigantic and new one. Toward what is known as evil, I lovingly pursued an adventure which led me to prison. Though they may not always be handsome, men doomed to evil possess the manly virtues. Of their own volition, or owing to an accident which has been chosen for them, they plunge lucidly and without complaining into a reproachful, ignominious element, like that into which love, if it is profound, hurls human beings...Repudiating the virtues of your world, criminals hopelessly agree to organize a forbidden universe. They agree to live in it. The air there is nauseating: they can breathe it.... (pp. 9-10)

I do not want to conceal in this journal the other reasons which made me a thief, the simplest being the need to eat, though revolt, bitterness, anger or any similar sentiment never entered into my choice. With fanatical care, "jealous care," I prepared for my adventure as one arranges a couch or a room for love; I was *hot* for crime. (*Ibid* p. 13)

This love informs my apostolate work—as love of neighbor should inform the ministry work with criminals undertaken by other Catholics—to try always to act in the spirit of the charitable love Pope Benedict XVI (2006) reminds us is at the heart of the Church.

The Church's deepest nature is expressed in her three-fold responsibility: of proclaiming the word of God (*kerygma-martyria*), celebrating the sacraments (*leitourgia*), and exercising the ministry of charity (*diakonia*). These duties presuppose each other and are inseparable. For the Church, charity is not a kind of welfare activity which could equally well be left to others, but is a part of her nature, an indispensible expression of her very being. (p. 60, #25a)

The moral judgments implicit within the hierarchy of evil have come down to current practice in the criminal/carceral world through corruption of the popular devotion, contemplation, and practice of teaching emanating directly from Christ—particularly in his relationships with the two proto-criminal saints, Mary Magdalene and Dismas—what he did as much as what he said.

The historic popular devotion of St. Dismas contributed to a development of criminal/carceral world doctrine still largely prevalent—protecting the innocent—through reflection upon Dismas' actions on Golgotha and on the Road to Egypt, where he protected the Holy Family from robbery and violence at the hands of his band of thieves.

The Catholic hierarchy of evil—venal sins, sins of moral gravity, and sins that cry out to heaven, is, as the *Catechism* states:

1854 Sins are rightly evaluated according to their gravity. The distinction between mortal and venial sin, already evident in Scripture, became part of the tradition of the Church. It is corroborated by human experience....

1867 The catechetical tradition also recalls that there are *"sins that cry to heaven"*: the blood of Abel, the sin of the Sodomites, the cry of the people oppressed in Egypt, the cry of the foreigner, the widow, and the orphan, injustice to the wage earner.

1868 Sin is a personal act. Moreover, we have a responsibility for the sins committed by others when *we cooperate in them*:

- by participating directly and voluntarily in them;
- by ordering, advising, praising, or approving them;
- by not disclosing or not hindering them when we have an obligation to do so;
- by protecting evil-doers. (#1854, #1867-1868)

Within the criminal/carceral world it is only some of these that are considered evil, though the hierarchy of evil within the criminal/carceral world is an adaptation of that which has been set by the Judea-Christian world through the Old Law and deepened and clarified by the New.

Beyond the validation of the Old Law by Christ, it is also in his other words and actions, especially in his relationship with the betrayer Judas and the Good Thief Dismas, that the root of the criminal world adaptation appears, which, down through the centuries has reconstituted itself into the hard reality that governs the internal narrative of criminals— and as the criminal perceives it—much of the internal narrative of the world upon which that of criminals is structured.

The sanctioning created and imposed by professional criminal prisoners against criminal/carceral world evils that exists inside maximum security prisons—which for the past several decades has also determined that of the outside criminal world—is an element congruent with the nature of the prison, as described by a former prisoner.

> County jail experiences and associations helped prepare me for my eventual journey into the California prison world of the 1970s. Still, the differences were dramatic. Jails are community facilities, close to family, where inmates serve short sentences. In comparison, prisons are places where people spend many years. The men, both prisoners and guards, are bigger and tougher, many with tattoos. Penitentiaries, maximum security "big

house" institutions are huge complexes, filled with thousands of men, and known for high levels of violence, blatant racism, and hatred....

The way I saw the world and myself continued to change during my early prison years. I became a lot like those I saw around me who seemed to be doing the easiest time. These were the guys who were respected; the ones with tattoos all over their bodies, lifting weights, drinking coffee with cream and sugar, smoking tailor-made cigarettes, getting high, and laughing all the time. My developing convict identity was learned from those men I associated with, the meanings we shared, the things we did, our use of language and prison humor, and how we were seen and treated by others. (Terry, 2003, p. 99)

The criminal/convict identity, built upon the necessity of survival in a brutal world where one mistake can mean death or horrible exploitation, is an identity that sticks, as former convict Irwin (1970) notes.

The convict identity is very important to the future career of the felon. In the first instance, the acquiring of the taken-for-granted perspective will at least obstruct the releasee's attempts to reorient himself on the outside. More important, the other levels of the identity, if they have been acquired, will continue to influence choices for years afterward. The convict perspective, though it may become submerged after extended outside experiences, will remain operative in its latency state and will often obtrude into civilian life contexts. (p. 84)

Each act of Christ in his ministry, in its continuance as a deep influence on human behavior—consciously or unconsciously—is vital. He set an archetype in his condemnation of the betrayal by Judas, that "it would have been better for that man if he had not been born" (Matthew 26:24). Though the great condemnation was directed specifically at Judas, its use against any betrayal has become normative within the world of the professional criminal and even within much of the noncriminal world.

A condemnation was also set against those who harm children. "...but whoever causes one of these little ones who believe in me to sin, it would be better for him to have a great millstone fastened round his neck and to be drowned in the depth of the sea." (Matthew 18:6) The condemnation remains today against pedophiles, who are subject to being killed if placed within the mainline of maximum security prisons.

Professional criminals define those who inform on their crime partners (a relationship within the criminal/carceral world of great trust, honor, and respect) or prey on innocent women and children, as decidedly evil, beyond the pale and unworthy of respect, in prison or out.

The sanctions against the evil of rapists and pedophiles, partially stems from criminals who do not even perceive those acts as deserving of the honor of being defined as a crime, as Carceral (2004) notes: "rape, pedophilia...are not perceived by prisoners as real crime." (p. 214)

Consequently, those acts are considered *outside* the morality of criminals and thus unable to expect protection within the normal bounds of respect within that world,

Some incidents legally defined as rape, such as statutory rape between two consenting individuals of similar age though one is legally under the age of consent, is not considered evil; though the violent serial rape of innocents is.

Informing is deeply hated: "ratting, snitching, telling, informing (a rat is hated by other inmates inside prison)", (*ibid.* p. 214) and can lead to death, as noted by clinical psychologist Dr. Stanton Samenow (1984).

> "Don't snitch" is a code among inmates. The price of squealing on another con may be a beating or even death. Even so, the inmate realizes that every man is out for himself and that even his best

buddy may turn informant to save his own skin or to acquire privileges. Although convicts share an understanding of "no snitching," the dominant ethos in prison, is, as it was outside, "Fuck everybody else but me." (pp. 145-146)

One type of outside criminal world informant situation, where a member of one criminal organization cooperates with law enforcement to effectively compete with a rival criminal organization by informing on them, is generally not considered a classical informant situation, but is generally defined as someone who corrupted law enforcement to satisfy personal criminal organizational goals.

The sanction within the criminal/carceral world visited upon sexual offenders and informers is marked by violence and goes much farther than that of the noncriminal community, which usually restricts its response, beyond the legal, to disgust and fear.

Professional criminals remember what the noncriminal world—including many rehabilitation practitioners—have forgotten (or perhaps criminals know what the practitioners do not know) that sexual predators and betrayers choose what they have done and are not acting because of corrosive familial or social influences and given the opportunity, will choose to repeat those acts.

Professional criminals understand the difference between the murder of one member of a gang by a member of another gang during a war for territory or profit (which is properly seen as an act of war soldiers are legitimately authorized to perform), and the murder of the child victim by a pedophiliac rapist, which is an act of the most predatory evil, and is more justly and severely sanctioned by professional criminals than most American criminal justice systems.

Capital punishment is the sentence professional criminals pronounce and execute upon child rapists, and this is where the misguided efforts by some Catholics to abolish capital punishment—a sanction which the historical tradition of the Church teaches as appropriate—conflicts with the conversion of criminals who would ask why a Church that does not understand the proper use of capital punishment is a Church for the ages.

Murder committed under the well known rubric, "It's just business" is considered by the criminal/carceral world as legitimate, while those committed on account of lust, thrill, or insanity, are not, as Machiavelli (1532) wrote:

> Those cruelties we may say are well employed, if it be permitted to speak well of things evil, which are done once for all under the necessity of self-preservation and are not afterwards persisted in... (p. 64)

Doing organized rehabilitation work that mingles those who, by criminal/carceral world standards, should be executed, with those who would perform or support the execution, is almost certainly guaranteed to fail, for it has exhibited a lack of understanding of a fundamental aspect of criminal/carceral world culture.

Criminals differentiate between informing on a crime partner and reporting to the police after having seen a violent crime committed against innocents—once having left the criminal life and become, in all respects, a regular citizen of the world.

The former is always evil, the latter is always good.

I would be remiss in not again mentioning the theory of radical criminology built on Marxism, which has set a different hierarchy of evil, one many prisoners have adopted as their way of perceiving their crimes, as Beirne & Messerschmidt (2000) write.

> Steven Spitzer devised probably the most intriguing Marxist theory of deviance. Assuming that capitalist societies are based on class conflict and that harmony is achieved through the dominance of a specific class, Spitzer reasoned that deviants are drawn from groups who create problems for those who rule. Although these groups largely victimize and burden people in their

own classes, "their problematic quality ultimately resides in their challenge to the basis and form of class rule". In other words, populations become problematic for those who rule when they disturb, hinder, or call into question any of the following:

1. capitalist modes of appropriating the product of human labor (called into question when the poor "steal" from the rich)

2. social conditions under which capitalist production takes place (questioned by those who refuse or are unable to perform wage labor)

3. patterns of distribution and consumption in capitalist society (questioned by those who use drugs for escape and transcendence rather than sociability and adjustment)

4. the process of socialization for productivity and nonproductive roles (questioned by youth who refuse to be schooled or those who deny the validity of family life)

5. ideology that supports the functioning of capitalist society (questioned by proponents of alternative forms of social organization) (pp. 198-199)

Richard Quinney added this in his Marxist theory on crime.

Quinney identified four types of crimes of domination that result from the reproduction of the capitalist system itself. "Crimes of control" include crimes by the police and the FBI... "Crimes of government" involve political crime..."Crimes of economic domination" consist primarily of corporate crimes...

"Crimes of accommodation" are acts of adaptation by the lower and working classes in response to the oppressive conditions of capitalism and the domination of the capitalist class...

Thus for Quinney, the crimes of domination seem to be the real societal harms, but they are not criminalized because they benefit the ruling class. Crimes of accommodation, on the other hand, range from simple adaptation to conscious political resistance. In fact, for Quinney, some crimes and, therefore, criminals are admirable elements in the overall class struggle. (*ibid.* p. 200)

This Marxist and sociological perspective informs many in the academy and has exerted great influence upon several criminals who have earned graduate and post-graduate degrees and secured positions in the academy, rendering rehabilitative pastoral ministry somewhat difficult because the theories and arguments are of some depth and resonate among those criminals who cherish the idea that their crimes have made them into heroes.

It is however, in the actions of the true criminal hero, St. Dismas, that the honor of the professional criminal was set. Dismas, the Good Thief, is portrayed as finding repentance hanging beside Christ on Calvary, but nothing in the scriptural record of that central moment in human history, as I read it, indicates that it was repentance he was expressing, but that he *saw* the truth.

Dismas *recognized* that the man hanging next to him *was* God. We do not know how he came to see this while so many others witnessing the crucifixion did not. It began perhaps on the Road to Egypt, where Dismas *really saw* love and innocence in the prototype family that he had perhaps dreamt of, but had not known.

In the act of saving the Holy Family from the robbing and violence characterizing his band of thieves, he acted benevolently for the same reason professional criminals today will not harm children, but will punish harshly—even unto death—those who do.

It was perhaps on the Road to Calvary, as the two thieves and Christ carried their crosses, as Dismas *saw* how others responded to Christ and him to them.

On the day of crucifixion Dismas *saw* the truth and remembered the episode on the

Road to Egypt, and his words to Christ were: "Jesus, remember me, when you come in your kingly power." (Luke 23:42)

Dismas might be saying: Remember that I have responded to you honorably, I have not pleaded for my life as Gestas—the other thief hanging on Golgotha—but have accepted my punishment honorably, for it is just. I have realized your innocence and know that while justice is being done with us, it is not being done to you, Jesus, "remember me."

This is not an unusual response for a professional criminal even today, for among ourselves in the cells and on the streets, we will openly and proudly acknowledge who we are, without remorse, asking for no mercy, and though trying any and everything to escape the consequences, once captured by judge and jury, we will accept our punishment stoically if the opportunity to escape is finally closed.

One of the elements in the hierarchy of evil, something that if a professional criminal expresses he will do, will result in him losing the trust and respect of other criminals, is claiming to desire to live a law-abiding life.

Criminals would react to this as would non-criminals react if a peer expressed becoming a criminal as a desired way of life—although in some circles the expression would only be seen as suspect if the criminal life being sought was one that had little chance of profit or success, so influenced has much of the public become to the blandishments of Hollywood and Marxism where criminals are as often seen as romantic figures than as evil predators.

Dismas *saw*—in the man hanging beside him—a man/God who was truly walking the talk, and living the truth under the most horrific of circumstances, the Roman crucifixion of criminals.

The decision by Christ to take Dismas into Hell with him—on the way to Paradise—is, from the human perspective Christ still possessed, a good and sound idea, as to take a criminal guide into the deepest lair of criminals, much as priests today might ask a reformed criminal to accompany him to a prison ministry visit, both for a sense-of-safety and credibility.

It is perhaps incongruous to think of Our Lord feeling the need for a guide, but on the other hand, it is congruent with his trepidation expressed in Gethsemane, and even on Golgotha, for he was still a man, subject to the human frailties which he would, however, soon leave behind him.

There are mysteries here I do not understand, but I know each act and each word of the earthy ministry of Christy has eternal meaning and all the books that could be written are being written and they do fill the world, but we are still mystified.

Part of the mystery is *why Dismas becomes* Christ's companion on the Road from Calvary to Paradise and in the process, becomes the first canonized saint of the

Catholic Church, and in response to this central question, Bishop Sheen (1958) writes.

> One would have thought a saint would have been the first soul purchased over the counter of Calvary by the red coins of redemption, but in the Divine plan it was a thief who was the escort of the King of kings into Paradise. If Our Lord had come merely as a teacher, the thief would never have asked for forgiveness. But since the thief's request touched the reason of His coming to earth, namely, to save souls, the thief heard the immediate answer: "I promise thee, this day thou shalt be with Me in Paradise." *Luke* 23:43. (p. 395)

In converting criminals, we should seek to understand this history and the related tradition of the Church regarding the protection of the innocent through the use of capital punishment and just war, so as not to fall into the avoidance technique that these are 'issues men of good will can disagree about'; for it is through sharing your understanding of the history and the tradition of protecting the innocent (as Dismas did on the Road to Egypt) that criminals will be able to see beyond the superficial uncertainties expressed by many Catholics around these traditional doctrines.

While the Church's current institutional approach to criminal justice is a somewhat depleted vessel—at least since the papacy of

Pius XII—the grounding of the Church's social teaching within the dogma of good and evil, still forms the axis around which the charitable and pastoral work of criminal rehabilitative ministry revolves.

The robustness with which charitable apostolate work must be done is noted by C.S. Lewis in a sermon he gave on June 8, 1941, entitled "The Weight of Glory", quoted by George Weigel (2008).

> There are no *ordinary* people. You have never talked to a mere mortal. Nations, cultures, arts, civilization—these are mortal, and their life is to ours as the life of a gnat. But it is immortals whom we joke with, work with, marry, snub, and exploit—immortal horrors or everlasting splendors. This does not mean that we are to be perpetually solemn. We must play. But our merriment must be of that kind (and it is, in fact, the merriest kind) which exists between people who have, from the outset, taken each other seriously— no flippancy, no superiority, no presumption. And our charity must be a real and costly love, with deep feeling for the sins in spite of which we love the sinner—no mere tolerance, or indulgence which parodies love as flippancy parodies merriment. Next to the Blessed Sacramento itself, your

neighbor is the holiest object presented to your senses. (p. 98)

The foremost author on criminal justice issues from a Catholic perspective, at the present time, is Dr. Andrew Skotnicki (2008), who wrote in the Acknowledgements section of his seminal book:

> Finally, I must say something about the countless men and women I have known in the jails, detention centers, and prisons of the United States. I beheld the face of God for over thirty-five years either as a volunteer, or as a part or full-time chaplain. Caregivers have said so often that they receive far more than they give that it has become a well-worn cliché, but it is a cliché precisely because over and over again, experience proves it to be true, and I feel deeply the joy and burden of gratitude to them all. (p. vii-viii)

In many ways, my life as a criminal and convict were some of the most important years of my life, for, as hard, as lonely, and as brutal as they so often were, surviving and thriving during those years gave me the experience that led to my apostolate work—as well as the foundation upon which I've found a peaceful, productive and fulfilling life—and it is in that work with professional criminals whose lives I've been part of during those many years past

113

and those of the still unfolding future, that I have also found work that God has called me to do.

Conclusion

While many Catholics have found great peace and happiness within the Church, the thought of evangelistically venturing into the terrifying world of the prison will often, especially in the beginning, somewhat hamper any resolve to do so, yet we can remember the great call to evangelization expressed so well by Lubac (1988).

> Have I found joy?...No, but I have found *my* joy and that is something wildly different....
>
> The joy of Jesus can be personal. It can belong to a single man and he is saved. He is at peace, he is joyful now and for always, but he is alone. The isolation of this joy does not trouble him; on the contrary: he is the chosen one. In his blessedness he passes through the battlefields with a rose in his hand....
>
> When I am beset by affliction, I cannot find peace in the blandishments of genius. My joy will not be lasting unless it is the joy of all. I will not pass through the battlefields with a rose in my hand. (p. 13)

No, you enter the battlefield with the great and ancient sword of the social teaching of the Church, and whether your work is within or outside of prison, it is a sword that will protect you and can free the prisoner.

While the work of the Lampstand Foundation has focused primarily on community reentry outside of prison, most faith based organizations working with prisoners do not focus much on the life of the prisoner after release from prison, which Johnson addresses (2008).

> As important as volunteer work within correctional facilities might be, it does not diminish the fact that reentry and aftercare tend to be largely overlooked by most religious volunteers and organizations. Compared to reentry, prison ministry is a much easier task to pursue and a safe service opportunity in what many consider to be an unsafe environment. Prisoners often appreciate the attention they receive from the outside world, and these exchanges tend to be overwhelmingly positive and nonthreatening for volunteers. Prison ministry, therefore, can be found in many U.S. congregations and among the thousands of religious volunteers who visit prisons every day. Likewise, faith-based organizations disproportionately opt for in-prison ministry rather than

out-of-prison services because reentry and aftercare are anything but easy or safe. For example, Prison Fellowship Ministries (PF), the largest faith-based prison ministry in the United States has always recognized that reentry and aftercare are vitally important, but PF's efforts have been only marginally involved in these areas. This oversight was recently acknowledged by PF President Mark Early, at a White House "Compassion in Action" Roundtable event on prisoner reentry in March 2007, when he stated an intention to remedy the imbalance by significantly expanding the organization's aftercare emphasis. (pp. 6-7)

During the 1970's and 1980's community based rehabilitation efforts were fairly substantial, with a lot of involvement from former criminals including myself, but after many years of substantial funding with virtually no success—though the program I developed and managed, as were a few others such as Delancey Street, successful—those slowly shut down.

Recently, through the Second Chance Act, funding for outside reentry programming has begun to open up again.

While the coming and going, success and failure, of outside prison reentry programs is common, it is my belief that the non-Catholic faith-based inside prison ministries will always fail, though individual stories of redemption will occasionally occur. The force of the argumentation their approaches take is key to their failure, while the slow and thoughtful revealing of Catholic history and social teaching principles allow for internal arguments, self-correcting change, and eventual *true* conversion to emerge, even given the deep sway the criminal/carceral culture exerts over its cohort's lives.

Mirus (2011, #2) writes:

> In classical apologetics, arguments proceed step by step toward something which at least approaches a proof. The arguments are important, but they cannot logically force someone to believe. If that were possible, then Faith would not be Faith. Rather, what classical apologetics is best at is clearing away mental obstacles to belief. The arguments demonstrate either that it is not unreasonable to believe this or that point of Christian doctrine, or that the ideas, perceptions and arguments we've used to buttress our non-belief will not pass close scrutiny.

> Typically a strong argument makes people feel vulnerable, and so it puts them on the defensive. While their defensive posture may change in private, in the silence of their hearts,

classical apologetics is essentially an adversarial enterprise. By its very nature it tends to buttress the confidence of the believer while minimizing any possible sympathy on the part of the non-believer. (Explanations in response to sincere questions, of course, may amount to the same thing but be exceedingly well-received.) Another problem with this sort of argumentative approach is that, in an age of pervasive media, we are so surrounded by constant argument that we have long since learned to discount it. Part of us fears that if we take arguments too seriously, we'll never be able to affirm anything.

People often confuse argument with assertion, but the problem remains. Nobody likes to be talked at, and most of us are very good at filtering out what we don't particularly want to hear. Even more to the point, few people find when they are not seeking. So there has to be a better way. (n.p.)

This is especially true of prisoners, so self-directed by nature, so rebellious by temperament, so resistant by experience, and so tempered by the world that anything driving change from outside is usually doomed in the long term and probably used to manipulate reality in the short.

119

The failure of most prison ministry efforts has played a role in the development of Lampstand's work to produce books and papers that may have some value in helping former prisoners become the type of leaders that can develop, manage, and sustain reentry programs in the community.

A major aspect in our books is to introduce the readers to other books through extended quotes from great writers who explain the eternal truths of Catholicism so much better than your author.

Books are the pathway to friendships with the immortals and through the many volumes of their works on earth, we can come to a companionship informing and enlightening our lives; and in this respect, perhaps the greatest of companions is the Angelic Doctor, St. Thomas Aquinas, whose works will enthrall you, challenge you and bring you into congruence with the ancient teachings of the Church like no other.

The failure of most prison ministry has also played a role in Lampstand making the decision to become involved in prison ministry.

While outside prison reentry work is seen as dangerous by the traditional volunteer, it is not so for the reformed criminal, in fact just the opposite. The bonding between criminals, who have shared experience in committing crimes for the purpose of making money, and consequently serving time in maximum security prison, is often long-lasting, and once the initial parameters are established about criminal and carceral pasts, the relationship between the penitential criminal and transformed criminal helper builds rather quickly.

This will not be true in prison ministry between the prisoner and the volunteer, but it can become true between the prisoner and the intellectual and historical works of the social teaching, between the prisoner and the lives and works of the saints and luminous Catholic thinkers such as Jacques and Raissa Maritain and Hilaire Belloc.

The prison minister has to be prepared to respond to questions about other religions and here the seminal books by Belloc, *The Great Heresies* and *How the Reformation Happened*, will be invaluable, as will the magnificent 2003 work by the Vatican Pontifical Council for Culture & Pontifical Council for Interreligious Dialogue: *Jesus Christ, The Bearer of the Water of Life: A Christian Reflection on the "New Age"*.

This discussion needs to be done in an intellectual, historical doctrinal comparison sense, without a lot of God-talk. The concepts of pacifism and socialism, which infects liberal Catholicism and weakens the histories of otherwise saintly Catholics like Dorothy Day, also needs to be addressed with a clear historical understanding of the traditional teaching of the Church about just war and the evil of socialism.

Pacifism has been part of the liberal Catholic history since the beginning—laying open fences to evil's run through human fields.

The criminal/carceral world is a hard, clear world of steel and stone and it will only be the crystalline purity of the eternal teaching of the Church that can strongly trump it, not the misty wishes of liberalism.

When I was in McNeil Island Federal Penitentiary in the 1960's, several draft resisters were sentenced there, most of whom were pacifists from the academies of the Northwest.

Criminals *despise* pacifists as they are the perfect victims, so out of touch with reality as to deserve no respect and so they were victimized and disrespected.

Combat theology—the theology of St. Thomas Aquinas, the Catholic Knights and kings and popes who fought with steel to protect Holy Mother Church—is theology that understands the mandate to protect the innocent and the defense of ourselves first of all; and that is the only theology that will take root in the criminal soul.

Pacifism concedes the ground to evil and injustice, thus the favorite deception of the devil—that the heart of Christ's teaching is pacifistic.

Love is the heart, love of God and neighbor. Surrender is at the heart, surrender to that divine love.

Pacifism is surrender to earthly evil, and to the beasts that look like men.

Upon these bones, transformation can begin to occur and "the great soul" of conversion "can emerge", as Barron (1998) writes.

> This book rests upon the conviction that real *metanoia*, the transition from a state of mind of fear to a mind of trust, is possible. Due to the playful, strange, unpredictable, and relentless love of God, the *imago* in us can be polished and the great soul can emerge. (p. 220)

Trust is at the root of faith; trust in what your mind and heart perceive beyond the obvious weight of the steel and stone prison world riven with evil, trust that the Kingdom of God exists even here, no less than in the open mountain meadows of our visions.

There are many men of good will in prison—this is something anyone who has worked with prisoners for any length of time already knows—but there are also many with the blackest of evil wills.

Determining between them is a key element of prison ministry, and here the teaching of Aquinas (1951) can be of help.

> Only that good which is complete in itself, and without need of supplement, is the good which the will is not able not to will. This is happiness. Other particular goods, in that they fall short

of some goodness, can be regarded as not good; as appreciated in that light they can be approved or rejected by the will, which can conduct itself in the same situation according to different points of view. (#700)

We will discover men of good will by their actions, not their words—as we do those of evil will—today and yesterday, particularly, within the details of the crimes they committed that brought them to prison.

St. Thomas understands, as Rickert (2011) writes:

> The will, according to St. Thomas, must intend good in order to fulfill its nature. In his mind, the will is an appetite; it is a power directed by nature to things understood, in one way or another, to be good. A good will should not, therefore, be seen as less free because it is "confirmed in the good." On the contrary, a will that is confirmed in the good is a will to ultimate goodness, fullness of being, perfection and power. The opposite of a good will is a weak will, a sick will, a will to weakness, imperfection, and negation of being and power. From a Thomistic point of view, the will that is detached from the ultimate good, the will that is not aimed at fullness of being and ultimate perfection, is powerless. It is a feeble

force that defies reason, lashing about in the dark, asserting its independence. It is like the "tale told by an idiot, full of sound and fury, signifying nothing" mentioned by Shakespeare's Macbeth. The will that is confirmed in the good, on the other hand, freely chooses fullness of being and perfection. (p. 69)

Penance encourages openness to evangelization, which can redeem the will and free it to act in its essential goodness, for the power of the *word* in that process is ultimate, as the *Catechism* teaches.

> **1122** Christ sent his apostles so that "repentance and forgiveness of sins should be preached in his name to all nations." "Go therefore and make disciples of all nations, baptizing them in the name of the Father and of the Son and of the Holy Spirit." The mission to baptize, and so the sacramental mission, is implied in the mission to evangelize, because the sacrament is prepared for by *the word of God and by the faith* which is assent to this word:
>
>> The People of God is formed into one in the first place by the Word of the living God. . . . The preaching of the Word is required for the sacramental

ministry itself, since the sacraments are sacraments of faith, drawing their origin and nourishment from the Word.

If your ministry is blessed by grace, and if, within the prison where you work, certain great souls emerge, there may be a time when you can direct them to the work of the spiritual director, Fr. Reginald Garrigou-Lagrange, O.P., who played a prominent role in the group around Jacques and Raissa Maritain, the influential evangelical Catholic couple who helped set in motion much of the reemergence of the modern devotion and study of St. Thomas Aquinas.

Fr. Lagrange's two volume work, *The Three Ages of the Interior Life* (1947) would be a sure guide for the advanced teaching of emerging prison monks and spiritual warriors, as this excerpt reveals.

In these questions [of spirituality] we have followed particularly three doctors of the Church who have treated these matters, each from his own point of view: St. Thomas [Aquinas], St. John of the Cross, and St. Francis de Sales. In the light of the theological principles of St. Thomas, we have tried to grasp what is most traditional in the mystical doctrine of *The Dark Night* by St. John of the Cross and in the *Treatise on the Love of God* by St. Francis de Sales.

We have thus found a confirmation of what we believe to be the truth about the infused contemplation of the mysteries of faith, which seems to us more and more to be in the normal way of sanctity and to be morally necessary to the full perfection of Christian life. In certain advanced souls, this infused contemplation does not yet appear as a habitual state, but from time to time as a transitory act, which in the interval remains more or less latent, although it throws its light on their entire life. However, if these souls are generous, docile to the Holy Ghost, faithful to prayer and to continual interior recollection, their faith becomes increasingly contemplative, penetrating, and full of savor, and it directs their action while making it ever more fruitful. In this sense, we maintain and we explain what seems to us the traditional teaching, which is more and more accepted today: namely, that the normal prelude of the vision of heaven, the infused contemplation of the mysteries of faith, is, by docility to the Holy Ghost, prayer, and the cross, accessible to all fervent souls. (p. vi)

The Lampstand prison ministry is evangelization using words, and when the words are from the sanctified teaching of the

Church, enhanced through the Sacramental Word and congruent with the history of the Church, the seeds of transformation for prisoners due to be released and actual transformation of prisoners serving natural life into spiritual warriors or prison monks able to literally change prison life from the inside out, is possible, as all things are possible through Our Lord.

There are many stories in the world but the one we know of Christ is true, which we must help criminals discover and defend.

The Church is always right and when she is not, God corrects her through the agency of others, whether they are evil, as Martin Luther of the Reformation or good, as Queen Elizabeth I of Protestant England.

Christ set the paradigm. Peter denied him and with the other apostles ran away at the climactic moment; save the apostle John, the Holy Virgin Mother, her sister Mary of Clopas, and Mary of Magdalene; but Peter is—as far as humanly possible—the Rock, and the contradiction is the truth we must always discern; for even as Peter stumbles how much more do we falter and fall. Forgive Peter, forgive our neighbor, forgive the criminal, yet serve justice as well.

Each detail, no matter how minor it might appear, in Christ's life, had meaning; and so it should be for our life of ministry; in each moment, in each act, in each thought we must attempt to create congruence with our apostolate for we cannot purpose an apostolate of love and truth to the world if we practice hate and lies at home and in our heart.

I have just finished watching the 1927, 155 minute version of the Cecil de Mille silent epic on the ministry of Christ, *King of Kings*, and it was the most beautiful presentation that I have ever seen; remarkable considering it was filmed over 80 years ago and is mostly black and white.

It opens in the courtesan Mary Magdalene's palace, filmed in brilliant color, and moves then to black and white, with several more bows to tradition, one being that the Holy Virgin Mother was the first to see the Risen Christ.

It is this combination of scripture and tradition from which we build the narrative of conversion and the building of this narrative comes from an immersion in Catholic teaching and history as portrayed in all of the venues the faithful have used throughout time.

Let us not forget the liturgy, which can play a central role in prisoner conversion and reformation.

As a convert—and still considering myself a novice Catholic—much of my study involves seeking the ancient roots of Catholic teaching and practice.

At many points during my Catholic journey I have been compelled to choose a particular path of further study.

The first was choosing conservative over liberal Catholicism, traditional teaching as expressed in the two universal Catechisms,

Trent & Vatican II, as opposed to that preached by the liberal wing of Catholicism.

The second was to seek guidance from Peter when uncertainties about Church teaching arose.

The liturgy is where we meet with God and seek to hear his quiet voice, but that took me years to truly understand, and our journey from our baptismal parish and liturgy to a Latin Mass parish has been an instructive one.

We were baptized into the Catholic Church at our home parish a few minutes drive from our house in 2004. It is a lovely and relaxed suburban parish run by the Jesuits and we happily attended mass there for a couple of years until becoming dissatisfied with its too liberal leanings being presented much too often through homilies, announcements, and events.

We attended several other parishes but encountered much the same problem. We were just about ready to give up and stay with our home parish when we heard about the Latin Mass parish pastored by the Priestly Fraternity of Saint Peter.

Our first experience of the Solemn High Latin Mass was one of awestruck delight, much like that felt at our first mass after baptism, but deeper and more resonating as the choir chanted, the priest incensed, and the packed parish seemed to pulsate with sanctity.

We became regular members and attended Sunday Mass there for a year or so.

Then my wife's work situation changed and she had to work Sundays. About the same time—this was in June 2008—I was feeling the call to begin attending daily mass and began re-attending our home parish, but the level of activity of the new mass was disconcerting though the liberal leanings were not so evident in the daily mass as the Sunday.

After about a year and a half a friend told me about his son who was a very orthodox Catholic priest who pastored a parish only a few minutes farther away and would I attend.

I did and was completely won over, so for a year or so I attended daily mass there, though still uncomfortable with the externality of the new mass compared to the internality of the old.

Peter, my ever faithful guide, captain of the great barque, writes:

> To express one of its main ideas for the shaping of the liturgy, the Second Vatican Council gave us the phrase *participatio actuosa*, the "active participation" of everyone in the *opus Dei*, in what happens in the worship of God. It was quite right to do so. The *Catechism of the Catholic Church* points out that the word "liturgy" speaks to us of a common service and thus has a reference to the whole holy People of God (cf. *CCC* 1069). But what does this active participation come down to? What does it mean that we

have to do? Unfortunately, the word was very quickly misunderstood to mean something external, entailing a need for general activity, as if as many people as possible, as often as possible, should be visibly engaged in action. However, the word, "part-icipation" refers to a principal action in which everyone has a "part". And so if we want to discover the kind of doing that active participation involves, we need first of all, to determine what this central *actio* is in which all the members of the community are supposed to participate. The study of the liturgical sources provides an answer that at first may surprise us, though, in the light of the biblical foundations considered in the first part, it is quite self-evident. By the *actio* of the liturgy the sources mean the Eucharistic Prayer. The real liturgical action, the true liturgical act, is the *oratio*, the great prayer that forms the core of the Eucharistic celebration, the whole of which was, therefore, called *oratio* by the Fathers. At first, simply in terms of the form of the liturgy, this was quite correct, because the essence of the Christian liturgy is to be found in the *oratio;* this is its center and fundamental form. Calling the Eucharist *oratio* was, then, a quite standard response to the pagans and to questioning intellectuals in general. What the Fathers were saying was this: The sacrificial animals and all those things that you had and have, and which ultimately satisfy no one, are now abolished. In their place has come the Sacrifice of the Word. We are the spiritual religion, in which in truth a Word-based worship takes place. Goats and cattle are no longer slaughtered. Instead, the Word, summing up our existence, is addressed to God and identified with *the* Word, the Word of God, who draws us into true worship. Perhaps it would be useful to note here that the word *oratio* originally means, not "prayer" (for which the word is *prex*), but solemn public speech. Such speech now attains its supreme dignity through its being addressed to God in full awareness that it comes from him and is made possible by him.

But this is only just a hint of the central issue. This *oratio*—the Eucharistic prayer, the "Canon"—is really more than speech; it is *actio* in the highest sense of the word. For what happens in it is that the human *actio* (as performed hitherto by the priests in the various religions of the world) steps back and makes way to the *actio divina*, the action of God. In this *oratio* the priest speaks with the I of the Lord—"This is my Body", "This is my Blood." He knows that he is not now speaking from his own resources but in virtue of the Sacrament that he has received, he has become the voice of Someone Else, who is now speaking and acting. This action of God, which takes place through human speech, is the real "action" for which all of creation is in expectation. The elements of the earth are transubstantiated, pulled, so to speak, from their creaturely anchorage, grasped at the deepest ground of their being, and changed into the Body and Blood of the Lord. The New Heaven and the New Earth are anticipated. The real "action" in the liturgy in which we are all supposed to participate is the action of God himself. This is what is new and distinctive about the Christian liturgy: God himself acts and does what is essential. He inaugurates the new creation, makes himself accessible to us, so that, through the things of the earth, through our gifts, we can communicate with him in a personal way. But how can we part-icipate, have a part, in this action? Are not God and man completely incommensurable? Can man, the finite and sinful one, cooperate with God, the infinite and Holy One? Yes, he can, precisely because God himself has become man, become body, and here, again and again, he comes through his body to us who live in the body. The whole event of the Incarnation, Cross, Resurrection, and Second Coming is present as the way by which God draws man into cooperation with himself. As we have seen, this is expressed in the liturgy in the fact that the petition for acceptance is part of the *oratio*. True, the Sacrifice of the Logos is accepted already and forever. But we must still pray for it to become *our* sacrifice, that we ourselves, as we said, may be transformed into the Logos (*logisiert*), conformed to the Logos, and so be made the true Body of Christ. That is the issue, and that is what we have to pray for. This petition itself is a way into the Incarnation and the Resurrection, the path that we take in the wayfaring state of our existence. In this real "action", in this prayerful approach to participation, there is no difference between priests and laity. True, addressing the *oratio* to the Lord in the name of the Church and, at its core, speaking with the very "I" of Jesus Christ—that is something that can be done only through sacramental empowerment. But participation in that which no human being does, that which the Lord himself and only he can do— that is equally for everyone. In the words of St. Paul, it is a question of being "united to the Lord" and thus becoming "one spirit with him" (1 Cor 6:17). The point is that, ultimately, the difference between the *actio Christi* and our own action is done away with. There is only *one* action, which is at the same time his and ours—ours because we have become "one body and one spirit" with him. The uniqueness of the Eucharistic liturgy lies precisely in the fact that God himself is acting and that we are drawn into that action of God. Everything else is, therefore, secondary. (Pope Benedict XVI (2000). (pp. 171-174)

We have since returned to the Latin Mass parish and the more I study and participate in the Latin Mass, the more certain I am that it can play a primary role—due to its constancy with the ancient roots of the Church—in the conversion of penitential criminals.

The past points towards the future for the prison ministry, as this from Geltner (2008) notes.

Largely as a response to their persecution under the Romans, early Christian apologists developed a basic imaginary of the prison. Martyrological narratives set in and around Roman jails introduced literary "sweet inversion" of despair into hope, of physical suffering into spiritual empowerment, and of secular coercion into divine grace. In this way, theodicy helped disseminate incarceration as a leitmotif of Christian spirituality, first among ascetics and later in monastic circles. As we shall see, self-imposed incarceration became a common metaphor for the angelic life and soon assumed purgatorial qualities. With one exception, which will be discussed below, the tie between prisons and purgation (and later, Purgatory) went on uninterrupted for more than a millennium.

The Martyrological literature conveying the experiences of Christian confessors presents the prison as a place of personal trial and eschatological triumph, and incarceration as a process of spiritual growth, potentially culminating in revelation. Thus, rather than precipitating apostasy, the harsh conditions of the Roman jail accelerated religious perfection: a classic "sweet inversion." In the emphatic words that Prudentius (348-405?) attributed to Fructuosus, the martyred bishop of Tarragona (d. 259),

> Prison to the Christian faithful is the path to glory,
> Prison propels to the heavens' summit,

Prison unites God with the blessed.

As a new locus of holiness, the prison attracted substantial attention from early Christians, whether laymen or clergy...

In the words of Tertullian (140-230): "The prison serves the Christian as the desert served the prophet...Even if the body is confined, even if the flesh is detained, everything is open to the spirit."

By comparing the prison with the desert, Tertullian linked Christian asceticism with the formative experiences of the Israelites and Christ's spiritual training....The metaphor subsequently found its way into monastic spirituality, which spawned a distinct new strand of carceral language. Thus, according to the Desert Mother Syncletica (d. ca. 400),

> In the world, if we commit an offence, even an involuntary one, we are thrown into prison; let us likewise cast ourselves into prison because of our sins, so that voluntary remembrance

may anticipate the punishment that is to come. (pp. 83-85)

The Lampstand vision of the future of criminal transformation within the Catholic Church envisions a host of sanctified and transformed professional criminals, who, through their acquisition of deep knowledge, will become heavily armed spiritual warriors, triple crowned professionals helping their brothers and sisters move from the criminal/carceral world to the communal world.

The tri-crowning comes from criminal world experience outside and inside a maximum security prison, postgraduate degrees from the academy, and advanced study in Catholic Social Thought, all fortified by a regime of daily practice: Ordinary or Extraordinary Mass or Divine Office, 15 Decade Rosary, Prayer and Contemplation.

Deep knowledge leadership is a going beyond a daily life of worldly dictated movement and moving to the supernatural symphony. It is the true way of the apostolate, drawing from a deep well of interiority strengthened by a lifelong pursuit of knowledge from the Fathers and Saints of the Church, *literally walking with Peter, to Christ, through Mary.*

Acquiring deep knowledge calls for a spiritual maturity earned through criminal experience, post-graduate education, and carceral suffering, a powerful octave in the way of perfection.

The way of perfection is congruent with entrepreneurial vision fused with spiritual knowledge, of those who have suffered, transformed their suffering, and can help others discover the path of transformation.

As criminals, we are people of the far edge, we must go to the maximum reach, for that is what draws us, and a rigorous daily practice built upon an ancient and formidable history and teaching, does and will draw us, it is the only foundation that will.

The 15 decade rosary will be among the primary tools in our arsenal—a powerful weapon—as St. Montfort (1954) teaches us:

> If you say the Rosary faithfully until death, I do assure you that, in spite of the gravity of your sins "you shall receive a never fading crown of glory" (p. 11)

For those who will remain in prison for the rest of their lives—and indeed, for the rest of us—the *Divine Office*, as Pope Paul VI, (1970) writes, is a great blessing.

> Public and common prayer by the people of God is rightly considered to be among the primary duties of the Church. From the very beginning those who were baptized "devoted themselves to the teaching of the apostles and to

the community, to the breaking of the bread and to the prayers" (Acts 2:42). The Acts of the Apostles give frequent testimony to the fact that the Christian community prayed with one accord.

The witness of the early Church teaches us that individual Christians devoted themselves to prayer at fixed times. Then, in different places, the custom soon grew of assigning special times to common prayer, for example, the last hour of the day, when evening draws on and the lamp is lighted, or the first hour, when night draw to a close with the rising of the daystar. (p. 8)

Lampstand envisions a legion of spiritual shock troops manning the front lines in the ancient war against evil, their souls flying the logos of Christ, their minds embracing the social teaching of the Church, their intellects wielding the sword of St. Michael, and in their hands, the 15 decade Rosary, the *Divine Office* and the *Catechism of the Catholic Church*, forming outposts in prison tiers, parish pews, neighborhood streets, and the halls of academia, united in seeking the reformation and transformation of their criminal brothers and sisters.

We will be penitential professional criminals—not informers, rapists, or pedophiles—men of honor retained in our world.

We will know that the only true path to freedom is internal—not mere provision of rehabilitative services—but growth from deep inside as knowledge and spirituality matures.

We will walk away from our criminal past, but not dishonor ourselves by revealing the who, when, and how of our past, throwing scraps of meat to the jailer from the table we once fed.

We will receive the forgiveness of baptism and our past will be cleansed.

We are called to be no less than saints and warriors within the great host in the eternal war against evil and the prince of this world, Special Forces shock troops in the legions of the mightiest angel in heaven, St. Michael the Archangel.

References

Adam, K. (1937). *The spirit of Catholicism.* (D. J. McCann, Trans.). Macmillan Company: New York.

Aquinas, St. Thomas. (1951). *St. Thomas Aquinas: Philosophical texts.* (T. Gilby, Trans.) New York: Oxford University Press.

Aquinas, St. Thomas. (1948). *St. Thomas Aquinas: Summa Theologica.* (Fathers of the English Dominican Province, Trans.) Notre Dame, Indiana: Christian Classics, Ave Maria Press.

Barron, R. (1998). *And now I see...A theory of transformation.* New York: Crossroad Publishing Company.

Beirne, P. & Messerchmidt, J. Jr. (2000) *Criminology.* Boulder, Colorado: Westview Press.

Beirne, P. & Messerschmidt, J. Jr. (2011) *Criminology: A sociological approach* (5th Ed.) New York: Oxford University Press.

Benestad, J.B. (2011). The Good Samaritan attends to every kind of suffering. *Fellowship of Catholic Scholars Quarterly, 34* (2). 54-55.

Bower. P. (2011, January-February) Briefly reviewed. [Review of the book *Pope Benedict XVI and the Sexual Abuse Crisis: Working for Reform and*

Renewal]. *New Oxford Review, 45,* 45-46.

Bureau of Justice Statistics (2010). *Recidivism, Summary Findings.* Retrieved June 24, 2010   from http://bjs.ojp.usdoj.gov/index.cfm?ty=tp&tid=17

Bureau of Justice Statistics (2011) *Prisoners at Year End 2009-Advance Counts.* Retrieved December 18, 2011 from http://bjs.ojp.usdoj.gov/content/pub/pdf/cpus10.pdf

Carceral, K. C. (2004). *Behind a convict's eyes: Doing time in a modern prison.* Belmont, California: Thomson Wadsworth.

Catechism of the Catholic Church. (1997). Retrieved April 24, 2010 from http://www.va/archive/ccc_css/archive/catechism/p3s2c2a7.htm

Crocker, H.W. III. (2001). *Triumph: The power and the glory of the Catholic Church—A 2,000 year history.* Prima Publishing: Roseville, California.

Engel, R. (2006). *The rite of sodomy: Homosexuality and the Roman Catholic Church.* Export, Pennsylvania; New Engel Publishing.

Euteneuer, T. J. (2010). Euteneuer Replies in Letters to Editor. *New Oxford Review.* May 2010. Retrieved June 10, 2010 from http://www.newoxfordreview.org/letters.jsp?did=0510-letters

Fairhurst, L. (2006). *FSU News*: Faith-based prison programs claim to reduce recidivism, but there's little evidence, says FSU research. Retrieved January 26, 2011 from http://www.fsu.edu/news/2006/10/04/prison.programs/

Gaume, Monsignor. (2003). [First published in 1882]. *Life of the good thief.* Fitzwilliam, New Hampshire: Loreto Publications.

Geltner, G. (2008). *The medieval prison: A social history.* Princeton: Princeton University Press.

Genet, J. (1964). *The thief's journal.* New York: Grove Press.

Guardino, R. (1956). *The Lord.* London: Longmans Green and Co LTD.

Hahn, S. Ed. (2009). *Catholic bible dictionary.* New York: Doubleday.

Hardon, J.A. *S.J.* (1999). *Modern Catholic dictionary.* Bardstown, Kentucky: Eternal Life.

Humphreys, C. *Sister, O.C.D.S.* (2011, February). Prayer as the heartbeat of the soul. *Homiletic & Pastoral Review, CXI,*(5), 22-25.

Irwin, J. (1970). *The felon.* Englewood Cliffs, New Jersey: Prentice-Hall, Inc.

Jenkins, H. W. Jr. (2011, March 12). The man who defined deviancy up. *The Wall Street Journal.* p. A13.

Johnson, B. R. (2008). The faith factor and

prisoner reentry. *Interdisciplinary Journal of Research on Religion, 4*(5), 1-21.

Lagrange, R.G. (1947). *The three ages of the interior life: Prelude of eternal life.* (Doyle, M. T. Trans.). St. Louis, Missouri: B. Herder Book Co.

Lewis, C. S. (2001). *The Screwtape letters with Screwtape proposes a toast.* San Francisco: Harper Collins Publishers.

Lubac, D. H. (1988). *Catholicism: Christ and the common destiny of man.* San Francisco; Ignatius Press.

Machiavelli, N. [1532] (2008) *The prince.* East Bridgewater, Massachusetts: Signature Press.

Maritain, R. (1936). *The prince of this world.* (G. Phelan, Trans.). Ditchling, England, St. Dominic's Press.

Maritain, J. (1968). *The peasant of the Garonne: An old layman questions himself about the present time.* (M. Cuddihy & E; Hughes, Trans). New York: Holt, Rinehart and Winston.

Maritain, J. (1996). (Bird. O. Ed.). *The collected works of Jacques Maritain, Volume XI: Integral humanism, Freedom in the modern world, and A letter on independence.* Notre Damc, Indiana: University of Notre Dame Press

Mears, D.P., Roman, C. G., Wolff, A., & Buck, J. (2006, July-August). Faith-based efforts to improve prisoner reentry:

Assessing the logic and evidence. *Journal of Criminal Justice.* *34*(4), 351-367.

Mirus, J. (2010). The Catholic publicity paradise. *Catholic Culture*, July 23, 2010. Retrieved July 26, 2010 from http://www.catholicculture.org/comme ntary/otc.cfm?id=676

Mirus J. (2011 #1). *Reforming criminals.* Catholic Culture January 11, 2011. Retrieved January 11, 2011 from http://www.catholicculture.org/comme ntary/otc.cfm?id=757

Mirus, J. (2011 #2). What this means: Christian witness in the modern world. *Catholic Culture*, February 24, 2011. Retrieved February 25, 2011 from http://www.catholicculture.org/comme ntary/articles.cfm?id=486

Montfort, L.M.D., St. (1954). *The secret of the rosary*. Bay Shore, New York: Montfort Fathers Publications.

Oxford Dictionary. (1993). *The new shorter Oxford English dictionary on historical principles*. (Brown, L. Ed.). Oxford: Clarendon Press.

Peters, E.M. (1995). "Prison before the prison: The ancient and medieval worlds", In Morris, N. & Rothman, D. J. Eds., *The Oxford history of the prison: The practice of punishment in Western Society* (New York: Oxford University Press.

Pearce, J. (1999). *Solzhenitsyn: A soul in exile.*

147

Grand Rapids, Michigan: Baker Books.

Pontifical Council for Justice & Peace. (2004). *Compendium of the social doctrine of the Church.* Vatican City: Libreria Editrice Vaticana.

Pope Benedict XVI. (2006). *God is love: Deus Caritas Est.* San Francisco: Ignatius Press.

Pope Benedict XVI (2000). *The spirit of the liturgy.* San Francisco: Ignatius Press.

Pope Benedict XVI. (Holy Week, 2010). (*Magnificat. 12* (1).

Pope John Paul II. (1991). *Centesimus Annus,* Papal Encyclical. Retrieved April 17, 2011 from http://www.vatican.va/edocs/ENG021 4/_INDEX.HTM

Pope Paul VI, (1970) *Christian prayer: The liturgy of the hours,* New York: Catholic Book Publishing Corp.

Rickert, K. G. (2011, February). The divine will and human freedom: A Thomistic analysis. *Homiletic & Pastoral Review, CXI* (5), 65-70.

Samenow, S. E. (1984). *Inside the criminal mind.* New York: Times Books.

Schuyler, K.G. (2004). *The Possibility of Healthy Organizations: Toward a New Framework for Organizational Theory and Practice.* Retrieved October 22, 2010 from http://coherentchange.com:8000/dox/ KGSchuyler-Possibility-of-Healthy-Orgs.pdf

Seward, D. (2000). *The monks of war: The military orders*. London: The Folio Society.

Sheen, F. J. (1958). *Life of Christ*. New York: McGraw-Hill Book Company, Inc..

Skotnicki, A. (2006). How is Justice Restored?, *Studies in Christian Ethics, 19* (2), 187-204

Skotnicki, A. (2008). *Criminal Justice and the Catholic Church*. New York: Rowman & Littlefield Publishers.

Sterling, C. (1994). *Thieves' world: The threat of the new global network of organized crime*. New York: Simon & Schuster.

Terry, C. M. *From c-block to academia: You can't get there from here*, in *Convict Criminology*, (Ross J. I. & Richards, S. C. Eds.). Belmont, California: Thomson Wadsworth.

Topping, R. (2011, January). The Catechism on how Catholics believe. *Homiletic & Pastoral Review, CXI*(4). 24-30

Useem, B. & Piehl, A. M. (2008). *Prison state: The challenge of mass incarceration*. New York: Cambridge University Press.

Weigel, G. (1987). *Tranquillitas ordinis: The present failure and future promise of American Catholic thought on war and peace*. New York: Oxford University Press.

Weigel, G. (2008). *Against the grain: Christianity and democracy, war and peace*. New York: Crossroad Publishing Company.

Weigel, G. (2010). *The end and the beginning: Pope John Paul II—the victory of freedom, the last years, the legacy.* New York: Doubleday.

Wilson, J. Q. & Herrnstein, R. J. (1985). *Crime & Human nature.* New York: Simon and Schuster

About the Author

David H. Lukenbill is a former criminal—thief and robber—who has transformed his life through education—an Associate of Arts degree in Administration of Justice from Sacramento City College, a Bachelor of Science degree in Organizational Behavior from the University of San Francisco, and a Master of Public Administration degree from the University of San Francisco—several years developing, managing, and consulting with criminal transformative organizations, and a conversion to Catholicism.

He is married to his wife of 28 years and they have one child. They live by the American River in California with three cats, and all the wild critters they can feed.

Contact information at the Lampstand Foundation website
www.lampstandfoundation.org

Prayer for Prisoners

✠ Divine Prisoner of the sanctuary, Who for love of us and for our salvation not only enclosed Yourself within the narrow confines of human nature and then hid Yourself under the veils of the Sacramental Species, but also continually live in the tabernacle! Hear our prayer which rises to You from within these walls and which longs to express to You our affection, our sorrow, and the great need we have of You in our tribulations - above all, in the loss of freedom which so distresses us.

For some of us, there is probably a voice in the depths of conscience which says we are not guilty; that only a tragic judicial error has led us to this prison. In this case, we will draw comfort from remembering that You, the most August of all victims, were also condemned despite Your innocence. Or perhaps, instead, we must lower our eyes to conceal our blush of shame, and beat our breast. But, even so, we also have the remedy of throwing ourselves into Your arms, certain that You understand all errors, forgive all sins, and generously restore Your grace to him who turns to You in repentance.

And finally, there are those among us who have succumbed to sin so often through the course of our earthly lives that even the best among men mistrust us, and we ourselves hardly know how to set out on the new road of regeneration. But despite all this, in the most hidden corner of our soul a voice of trust and comfort whispers Your words, promising us the help of Your light and Your grace if we want to return to what is good.

May we, o Lord, never forget that the day of trial is an opportune time for purifying the spirit, practicing the highest virtues, and acquiring the greatest merits. Let not our afflicted hearts be affected by that disgust which dries up everything, or by that distrust which leaves no room for brotherly sentiments and which prepared the road for bad counsel. May we always remember that, in depriving us of the freedom of our bodies, no one has been able to deprive us of freedom of the soul, which during the long hours of our solitude can rise to You to know You better and love You more each day.

Grant, O Divine Savior, help and resignation to the dear ones who mourn our absence. Grant peace and quiet to this world which has rejected us but which we love and to which we promise our co-operation as good citizens for the future.

Grant that our sorrows may be a salutary example to many souls and that they may thus be protected against the dangers of following our path. But above all, grant us the grace of believing firmly in You, of filially hoping in You, and of loving You: Who, with the Father and the Holy Spirit, live and reign forever and ever. Amen.

O Sacred Heart of Jesus, make us love Thee more and more!
Our Lady of Hope, pray for us!
Saint Dismas, the Good Thief, pray for us!

by Pius XII, April 1958

Prayer to St. Dismas

Glorious Saint Dismas, you alone of all the great Penitent Saints were directly canonized by Christ Himself; you were assured of a place in Heaven with Him *"this day"* because of the sincere confession of your sins to Him in the tribunal of Calvary and your true sorrow for them as you hung beside Him in that open confessional; you who by your love and repentance did open the Heart of Jesus in mercy and forgiveness even before the centurion's spear tore it asunder; you whose face was closer to that of Jesus in His last agony, to offer Him a word of comfort, closer even than that of His Beloved Mother, Mary; you who knew so well how to pray, teach me the words to say to Him to gain pardon and the grace of perseverance; and you who are so close to Him now in Heaven, as you were during His last moments on earth, pray to Him for me that I shall never again desert Him, but that at the close of my life I may hear from Him the words He addressed to you: "This day thou shalt be with Me in Paradise." Amen.

Prayer to St. Michael for Protection of the Catholic Church and Her Members

✠ Glorious St. Michael, Guardian and Defender of the Church of Jesus Christ, come to the assistance of the Church, against which the powers of Hell are unchained. Guard with thy special care her august visible head, and obtain for him and for us that the hour of triumph may speedily arrive.

✠ Glorious Archangel St. Michael, watch over us during life, defend us against the assaults of the demon, assist us especially at the hour of death, obtain for us a favorable judgment and the happiness of beholding God face to face for endless ages. Amen

www.ingramcontent.com/pod-product-compliance
Lightning Source LLC
LaVergne TN
LVHW021458080426
835509LV00018B/2330